SECRETS

TO YOUR

SUCCESSFUL
DOMESTIC
ADOPTION

Insider Advice to Create
Your Forever Family Faster

JENNIFER JOYCE PEDLEY
Birthmother and Social Worker

Health Communications, Inc.
Deerfield Beach, Florida

www.hcibooks.com

Library of Congress Cataloging-in-Publication Data

Secrets to your successful domestic adoption : insider advice to create
   your forever family faster / Jennifer Joyce Pedley.
       p. cm.
   Includes bibliographical references and index.
   ISBN-13: 978-0-7573-1468-1
   ISBN-10: 0-7573-1468-6
   1. Adoption—United States.   I. Title.
HV875.55.P43 2010
362.7340973—dc22

                                                            2010029567

HCI, its logos, and marks are trademarks of Health Communications, Inc.

Publisher: Health Communications, Inc.
          3201 S.W. 15th Street
          Deerfield Beach, FL 33442–8190

Cover design by Justin Rotkowitz
Inside design and formatting by Dawn Von Strolley Grove

This book is dedicated to

my brave birthmother sisters everywhere . . .

even if no one else does, you know who you are.

"Grown-ups never understand anything for themselves,
and it is tiresome for children to be always
and forever explaining things to them."

—Antoine De Saint-Exupéry

Contents

Part III: Using Your MBA (Marketing for Baby's Adoption)

Part IV: No, This Isn't Baseball
(As You Can See from All the Crying)

Part V: Unlike a Highway, a Pet, or a Tree,
This Adoption Is Forever

Acknowledgments

Almost twenty years ago, I found my life's work in the most unexpected way possible. I thank God for all the amazing people I have in my life. Without them, not only would I be an entirely different person, this story would be too.

I wish to thank Kenny, the love of my life and sharer of my head. I could never have made it this far without you. Without your good heart, level head, and strong coffee, I'd be lost. Wanna grow old with me?

I wish to thank my beautiful baby boys, Asher and Isaac. Being your mama has been just what the doctor ordered. You two smart, creative, and adorable creatures were more than worth the wait. I love you both!

A big thank-you goes to my editor, Allison Janse, for listening to my crazy ideas and then still keeping me on track. I would also like to thank Shelley Ballard, my favorite all A's attorney, for all of her very "schmarty" advice; Maggie Benz and Tobi Ehrenpreis for teaching me everything I know about adoption (especially the part about integrity always winning); Cher, for all of her late-night cheerleading (I love you, Mother Earth!); Debra, for waaay too many years of always believing in me; and Sheryl, for not being surprised at all.

I am surrounded by such love and support I couldn't possibly name each source. Beth, Kris, Gayle, and Trish—the four other Joyce girls—I'm glad none of you were boys! I am so lucky to have two sets of parents who love me, and even luckier that I'm just as much at ease referring to my in-laws as "Mom and Dad" as I am my mom and dad. To everyone from 2|42, to those cheering from Illinois, and our dearest friends the Wares—I love you guys!

Finally, I would like to extend thanks to everyone who has ever given a dime to the On Your Feet Foundation. Thank you, sincerely, for supporting such a worthy cause in a time when there are so many worthy causes worth supporting. To every adoptive family I've known, it is an honor to have been a little part of your family's story, and to the amazing birthparents who played a much bigger part than I, this is all for you.

Finally, to Ron, Sybil, Marcus, and Grey: Twenty years ago you all became family; saying "thank you" doesn't even begin to express what it means that for not one moment did you question what was meant to be.

Introduction

When a former client remarked to me after completing his adoption, "You know, there is a book to be written here," I thought, *Yeah, that's an understatement!* Although I kept my response to myself, my reaction was due mostly to the fact that I had already been writing about this subject, almost constantly in some way, shape, or form, for nearly twenty years. Beginning with my own journal that I kept during my pregnancy and days following my son's adoption process right up to that very week of receiving his comment, I had gotten into the habit of writing down my many thoughts and feelings about adoption before they flew out of my brain, never to be seen again! What I had was not even close to a book, but a mishmash of often-ineloquent hyperbole.

Narrowing down which things "needed to be said" was in many ways much harder than saying them. I have tried to gather all the things that, over the years, have been so obvious to me, but were always huge aha moments for all the clients I've worked with. Being both a birthmother and a social worker has enabled me to have a unique view of the adoption process that few others can see. Having helped so many courageous women (and men) go through the adoption process, and having been there myself, has taught me that this process never ever becomes routine and can never be treated as such. Every seemingly insignificant action causes a wave of reaction that extends far beyond the people on the front lines.

As you read the book, you'll probably realize that there are some things related to this topic that I don't talk about very much. For one, I don't discuss birthfathers specifically. This isn't because I don't think they are valuable and that there isn't a great deal that should be said about birthfathers, but honestly, that is the exact reason I chose to not dissect that topic in detail. There is too much that needs to be said, and to cover birthfathers too briefly would only do them a disservice.

I use the word "birthmother" or "birthparent" interchangeably in this book but occasionally have felt the need to add "birthfather" to the list as well. Please don't take this as meaning birthfathers are only important in those instances or shouldn't be included in every other mention; I just didn't feel I could tackle that subject and do it justice.

I also refer to the people who adopt children as "prospective adoptive families," "adoptive families," or sometimes just "families." Where I feel it is important to refer to women who are still pregnant as "expectant mothers" because they are not yet "birthmothers," I did not feel the same strong pull to differentiate between people who had not yet adopted and those who had, I guess partially because writing "prospective adoptive parents" every time I referred to you would have quickly become maddening (both to write and to read!). I apologize to anyone who finds this discriminatory, as this was certainly not my intention.

Every story in this book is true. Most names have been changed and some periphery details of stories have been altered to make them less recognizable when appropriate, but all the major themes and lessons learned come from actual experiences I've had while working in the field of adoption or from the people I know personally.

Research has now proven that both birth and adoptive families benefit from sharing information and maintaining a personal connection throughout an adopted child's life. Most people in the adoption community see this approach as a welcome change. Less secrecy and more openness is always good, if you ask me. It must have been a wise person who first said, "We are only as sick as our secrets"! If the goal is for adoption to be a decision that birthmothers can be proud of, and adoptive families can be completely at ease with, then I think we are moving in the right direction.

I am confident the steps I've outlined here will help you adopt more quickly and with less anxiety. I have a unique and advantageous perspective because I approach every step with both my professional training and education (in order to "know better"), as well as relying on my personal experience as a birthmother (which certainly helps me to "do better"). I have spent as much time in the delivery room as I have in the courtroom. I've become a pro at building a great "Dear Birthmother" letter, primarily after empathizing with hundreds of expectant mothers agonizing over who should raise their baby. My hope is that by sharing these insights, you too will not only experience the adoption process without the usual anxiety and fear, but also gain the confidence you need to be an intelligent ambassador of adoption for your child.

Please don't consider my book to be the complete resource on adoption by any means, but rather just one "specialty store" among a long list of others that you should visit. I would love to tell you that my book is the one and only "magic bullet" you'll need to adopt and raise the perfect adopted child, but that may be a little pompous, even for me! I have many amazing colleagues in this field who I respect and admire, and it would be ridiculous for me to say that their work isn't valuable too. Although, without my book, your adoption journey will absolutely lack the efficiency and understanding it could otherwise have. Through reading this, you will learn that laughing and crying, often at the same time, is not only normal in adoption, it is also expected! I do hope that this book will help you experience more of the joys and less of the tears along your journey, wherever that journey may lead.

Part I
Second Choice/Second Best

1

The Case for Domestic Adoption

It isn't uncommon for couples to tell me that when they began investigating adoption, they never even bothered to include infant domestic adoption in their research. They simply believed that it wasn't a realistic or affordable way to bring a child into their home. Many people believe that if they are over a certain age, already have biological children, are unmarried, are gay, or are just too plain dull, they will never be chosen by a birthmother to adopt her baby. I'm here to say this just isn't true (and I know many, many families from each of the above categories who can prove that I know what I'm talking about!).

Adoptive Families magazine reported that in 2007 there were an estimated 25,000 infant adoptions in the United States, while there were only 21,600 international adoptions. A reader's poll of the same year indicated that 56 percent of those families who adopted domestically completed their adoptions in six months or less, and a whopping 78 percent took only twelve months or less. These numbers reveal that the reality of domestic adoption in the United States contrasts starkly with what most people believe to be a legally risky and extremely lengthy process.

Since my own son's birth and adoption plan in 1990, I have met hundreds of parents who have built their families using various methods and means of adoption. I love hearing people's adoption stories, partially because no two are the same, but also because it is the sharing of, quite possibly, the most sacred journey of their lives. Most of the time, if they hadn't told me first, I would have just assumed they were genetically related (just like everyone else probably does). Hearing their stories is like receiving a little gift, one that most people don't unwrap for just anyone who happens to ask, and so I consider myself fortunate.

Domestic infant adoption remains the most frequent type of adoption Americans use to build their families. This has happened despite the fact that the average person knows very little about the process and continues to believe the all-too-common misconceptions. Here are the top three reasons I believe domestic adoption remains a mystery to most people:

HIDING IN PLAIN SIGHT

Domestic adoptions most often do not create conspicuous families, meaning that the members of a family often resemble each other, or are at least of the same racial makeup. Statistics from the U.S. Department of Health and Human Services reveal that same-race placements still make up a great majority of infant domestic adoptions in the United States. People more often recognize internationally adopted children (excluding Caucasian children from Eastern Europe) because they don't "look like" their parents or siblings. People observing these families may ask what I call "grocery store questions," such as "Oh, where did you get her?" or "What is he?" which create awkward moments that require an adoptive parent to have some prerehearsed responses that will hopefully explain, as well as educate, the obviously ignorant inquirer.

Of course, an adorable newborn baby adopted domestically might generate some grocery store curiosity as well, but if some busybody comments on how remarkable it is that you've lost all your pregnancy weight so quickly, my advice is to forget the adoption educating—just smile and say, "Why, thank you!"

SUCCESSFUL ADOPTION DOESN'T MAKE HEADLINES

The second reason Americans know very little about domestic adoption is because we see very few realistic examples of the common "happy ending" adoption process in the media. Our culture eats up the sensationalized and the tragic as fast as it is fed to us, and adoption is no exception. Just as horrific murders garner media attention over feel-good human interest stories, the rare con artist posing as a birthmother makes the news over the selfless birthmother who fully embraces the cooperative adoptive process.

THIS ISN'T YOUR FATHER'S ADOPTION

The third reason most people are in the dark about domestic adoption is because the process has changed rapidly in a relatively short period of time. Unless you've been personally involved in adoption in the past twenty years, it will probably surprise you how different the process looks today.

Infant domestic adoption in this new millennium creates a cooperative, empowered environment where everyone involved comes together and considers the child's needs first and foremost. We've moved from completely closed adoptions, when no identifying information was exchanged between parties, to today, when, according to one study conducted by the Evan B. Donaldson Adoption Institute, 90 percent or more of women who made voluntary adoption plans for their children met the adopting parents face-to-face, and the birthmothers who didn't meet the parents assisted with the selection process of the family through profiles.

With the publication of longitudinal studies like the Minnesota/Texas Adoption Research Project (MTARP), we now have scientific evidence supporting the hypothesis that open adoption, defined as an adoption in which direct contact between an adopted child and his or her birth family is regular and ongoing, offers benefits for all members of the adoption triad. Adopted children are less preoccupied with the concept of being adopted, birthparents are able to experience a more fully resolved grieving process, and adoptive parents feel more secure in their parent-child relationships.

Adoption Success Story:
When Truth Really Is Better Than Fiction

IT WAS A BEAUTIFUL AUTUMN WISCONSIN DAY, cool enough to need a wrap but warm enough to leave my coat in the car. I gripped my husband's arm tightly and stepped deliberately in my heels, careful to land squarely in the middle of the slate patio pavers, kittywhompus from years of frost and thaw. There wasn't exactly an aisle, but we sat down in the chairs on the left anyway, the side traditionally filled by guests of the bride. Even though it was nearly sixteen years since my own wedding, I am not ashamed to admit that, like most chicks, I still get butterflies in my stomach just before any bride appears on her own big day. In the case of this particular bride, I was weepy before we even sat down in the fairy-tale courtyard. All weddings are significant, but this wedding was especially sweet to me because the bride was my dear friend Rikki, a birthmother who I first met only weeks after she had given birth to her daughter, Lena, and had gently placed her into the arms of her new adoptive family.

In an odd sort of way, I felt a surge of pride, as if I, the mother hen, was watching one of my baby chicks leave the nest. I had watched Rikki "grow up" in the last seven years (probably more than she had in the previous twenty!). She was a part of the first group of birthmothers to whom I'd become an unofficial mentor, adviser, and cheerleader through years of their open adoption journeys. Many others in that very group of remarkable women were sitting around me as well; I could almost feel them absorbing the hope that they too would find happiness in their own lives. Certainly, a wedding is a big step for anyone, but for a birthmother who wonders every day how her life will play out differently because of that crossroad decision, it is a giant leap!

Lena, now seven years old, emerged from behind the ancient stone columns and began to make her way toward the front, her fancy princess dress swishing with each step. As she tossed pink rose petals from a dainty basket, I wished that I could somehow bottle this moment to replay for every apprehensive pre-adoptive couple I'd ever tried to convince of the benefits of open adoption. It's one thing to read about it in a book or to hear about it from an "expert" at an adoption conference, but completely another to see it being lived out with Technicolor emotions.

Next down the aisle were Rikki's two sisters, followed by the third and final member of the wedding party, the matron of honor. Nothing unusual there, except that Rikki's matron of honor, Nancy, is also Lena's adoptive mother. If you knew Rikki and Nancy, you wouldn't be surprised. After all, they've been family since the day Lena was born. I'm still not sure what is more wonderful: that Rikki had the honor of having her daughter be a part of that monumental day or the fact that Lena had absolutely no idea what a remarkable thing it was for her, her mom, and her birthmom to all be standing there. After all, this was just normal life for her—nothing unusual to be surrounded by all the people who love her.

2

Choosing the Least Bad Choice

In April 1990, I was twenty years old, in my third year of college, and about four months pregnant when I came to the conclusion that making an adoption plan for my baby was the least bad choice for my life. I had ruled out abortion weeks before and was left with sorting out the implications of either having a baby and being a mother for the rest of my life or having a baby and asking someone else to be the mother for the rest of both our lives. Either way, I was having a baby, and that wasn't a choice that could ever be undone.

The minute—no, the second—I found out I was pregnant, my life was changed forever. The reality of any unplanned pregnancy is that you have three choices. If you decide not to choose . . . well then, guess what? You just chose. No matter what, you will never be the same person ever again. Of course, I didn't recognize that then, but I certainly know it now. To me, none of my options were ones I wanted. And so, I soon decided that adoption was the least bad choice for me and the best choice for my baby.

Up to that point, I wasn't thinking about the family who would adopt my child. I could only focus on getting through the spring semester. That meant hiding my pregnancy from the nine sorority sisters I lived with—not easy! I had an inconvenient tendency to go from feeling perfectly well one second to puking in the bushes the next, I regularly fell sound asleep in the library when I should have been reading Homer's *Odyssey*, and—probably the hardest thing of all—I felt like sobbing all the time. I had absolutely no energy to think about anyone's needs except my own! Right then, my decision to not parent my son was based solely on my own needs, not at all on the needs of my future child. Having three sisters, all older and married with children (one only a newborn), I understood, at least in a pragmatic way, what it meant to be a mother. I had witnessed up close and personal what it was like to have the responsibility of a crying, pooping, awake-all-night newborn who had the power—and wasn't afraid to use it—to make you a captive in your own home.

When I was younger and offered to babysit my nephew, my sister most often opted not to go to a movie but to take a nap. It wasn't until after my son was actually born that I was really able to understand the magnitude of the concept of motherhood, but during my early pregnancy, my biggest thought was just how much a baby would interrupt my social life.

Once I had settled on the plan of adoption, I next faced telling my parents I was pregnant. Honestly, the idea to not tell them had never even crossed my mind, although now I wonder why it didn't. Maybe because even though I was a twenty-one-year-old grown woman on the outside, inside I was still a little girl who wished her mommy could rescue her.

My parents grew up in the 1940s and 1950s, a time when secrets were preferred (if given a choice), and what the neighbors thought of you was almost more important than who you really were. Raised in a conservative "churchgoing" part of the country, I even attended a small Christian college when I got pregnant. I was expected to always look good on the outside regardless of how I felt on the inside, but soon that would be impossible for even me to pull off. Yeah, it's pretty hard to hide what your insides look like when they are suddenly your outsides!

My mother's response to my news was quite practical and matter-of-fact. She would help in any way she could—I think she meant monetarily—but she had raised her children and she did not plan to raise her grandchild too. As cold as that sounds, I am so thankful for my mother's frankness. In the days after my son's birth, when more than anything in the whole world I wanted to cave in to the most natural and powerful force on Earth—the agonizing pull of motherhood—and completely change my plans, I heard my mother's voice in my head. As strong as the instinct was to hold my baby in my arms *now*, I somehow still knew that he needed more than I had to offer. Underneath my mother's words was the message that I, alone, would be the mom. Me, and no one else. The enormity of that reality was simply overwhelming.

My father, on the other hand, clearly preferred that I get married and pretend to live happily ever after, like so many other people in our family had already done successfully (that is, if you were only looking at their outsides). While I know my father was embarrassed by the whole situation, I have long ago forgiven him for that; after all, he was certainly a product of the times in which he was raised too.

Marrying my child's birthfather was never an option I seriously considered. I wasn't in love with him, he was graduating in May, and he had a job all lined up. When I told him I was pregnant, he immediately pointed out that many of his close friends were also my close friends, and how would they not find out? Obviously, he was raised in the same fine cultural tradition of secrecy as I was.

With no intention to marry, my adoption plan was the first major decision I had ever made based solely on my own needs (and later, the needs of my baby) and not on what anyone else wanted or expected of me. My decision to make an adoption plan for my son—that single decision—served as the major catalyst in my life for personal growth and direction. From that day forward, I stood on my own two feet in a different way.

3

Fertility:
Too Much or Too Little
(Either Way, a Big Problem)

B elieve it or not, adoptive parents and birthparents have a great deal in common. Unfortunately, it usually isn't until after an adoption is complete that you may see it. Adoptive parents are like the yin to the birthparents' yang: completely opposite, yet without each other, neither can be complete.

In a perfect world, no one would need adoption. People would get pregnant when they wanted and would not when they didn't. Despite the flowery language people use, including calling adoption a "gift" or a "selfless treasure," the not-so-flowery truth is that adoption is rarely anyone's first choice. If you are feeling adoption is your "least bad choice," as I did twenty years ago, then you are feeling exactly what anyone would feel in your shoes. Don't worry though, I promise you won't always feel this way. If you aren't there already, someday those thoughts will be replaced with a simple knowledge that we all get the children we are meant to have—however we get them.

I have never—not one day—regretted my decision to make an adoption plan for my son. Of course, I wish I could have given birth to him ten years later when I was ready, but that desire is very different from regret. I never dreamed of having a baby for someone else, nor do most adoptive mothers dream of needing someone else to enable them to have children. Dream or not, we certainly do help each other!

When most people first approach the idea of adoption, they have no idea what to expect. Even if they have a family member or friend who adopted a child, the adopting parent probably didn't share the nitty-gritty details of the entire process, so it remains somewhat of a mystery to most people. Many people go into adoption with the notion that adoption is like a game of sports. There are two teams, the adoptive parents on one side and birthparents on the other, and in the middle, acting as the referee, is the agency or an attorney. Maybe you picture the agency to be more like a coach, blowing a whistle and directing both sides. If that's your impression, there is good reason for it. Start reading any adoption agency website, and you will find phrases like, "choose a family who has been carefully screened by our agency staff" or "your assigned adoption counselor will carefully guide you through the process." Words like "screened" and "assigned" definitely give the clear picture of who's calling the plays.

Sometimes a family may feel they have no control at all, but rather it's the birthmother who holds all the power. American Adoptions, one very large adoption agency, lists the following paragraph in the section of its website intended for expectant mothers, "Today's adoption process is very much like a road trip—the birth mother is in the driver's seat, choosing which road to take, how fast to go and is even free to stop and get out of the car whenever she wishes. The adoptive family is in the backseat, going along for the ride with the birth mother, but not having any control over the trip itself."

Whoa! That doesn't really sound like a ride I would sign up for. Clearly this agency wants expectant mothers to understand that they have choices, and wants the pre-adoptive couples to understand that they do not have control over the birthmother's decision on whether or not to place. While legally true, I propose—and know from personal and professional experience—that the adoption process works far better and benefits everyone when everyone works together.

In reality, an expectant mother may feel like she is the one in the backseat and someone else is doing the driving. If she decides she does want out of the car, she often feels that her only option is to jump from the moving vehicle or sneak out when no one is looking.

Depending on the situation, she might perceive that the adopting couple has control or the agency or attorney has the steering wheel and controls the direction of the trip. One birthmother told me that she felt like it was her mother driving the car, and both she and the adopting couple were hanging on for dear life! Herein lies the biggest problem with any of these situations. If everyone perceives someone else is in control, then who is really driving the car?

Fear, loss, and fear of losing control obscures the adoption process. Adoptive parents are terrified to talk on the phone to expectant mothers, and expectant mothers are terrified to make the call. Adoptive parents are afraid that an expectant mother won't ever choose them; expectant mothers have incredible anxiety that the adoptive parents will find a better situation and dump them midstream. Adoptive parents are nervous that the new mother (not yet a birthmother, as there has not yet been an official adoption placement made) will see her baby and change her mind; expectant mothers imagine the adoptive parents may reject their baby because of an unforeseen medical issue or because of how the baby looks. When the baby arrives, both parties may feel insecure and believe the person sitting across from them has everything they wish they had.

But neither the adoptive parents nor the expectant mother needs to feel this way. By examining a model I call "The Parallel Lines of Adoption," adoptive parents and birthmothers can "see" the losses and fears that run parallel for everyone involved.

THE PARALLEL LINES OF ADOPTION

The figure below shows examples of the birth and adoptive mothers' fears and losses plotted on two parallel lines. Although the experiences occur at different points in time (which is why they cannot share just one timeline but require two), and they are not exactly the same (which is why the lines are parallel and will never intersect), for every loss or fear plotted on the line belonging to the birthmother, there is a comparable feeling experienced by the adoptive mother as well. Check off the feelings that apply to you, and feel free to add or subtract from the list of experiences to tailor the exercise to your personal situation. Review the experiences for both the adoptive mother and the birthmother; you'll see you are not alone with your fears.

The Parallel Lines of Adoption

An Adoptive Mother . . .	A Birthmother . . .
• feels a loss of control over her body and her fertility.	• feels a loss of control over her body and her fertility; distinctly true when birth control methods failed.
• may feel that her lack of fertility is a divinely ordained punishment.	• may feel that anything bad that happens in her life is a divinely ordained punishment for her unplanned pregnancy.
• grieves the loss of experiencing pregnancy and of giving birth.	• grieves the loss of enjoying and celebrating her pregnancy and birth. Will find that subsequent, even planned pregnancies will be mixed with sadness.
• may experience anger or jealousy when friends and family are able to conceive with ease.	• may experience anger or jealousy when others are successful in carefully planning their pregnancies.

An Adoptive Mother . . .	A Birthmother . . .
• may find it difficult to be around pregnant women or newborn babies.	• may find it difficult to be around pregnant women or newborn babies.
• may never parent a child who resembles her.	• sees a child who resembles her but who she will never parent.
• feels she doesn't fit with the other new mothers who talk endlessly about labor, delivery, and breast-feeding.	• will be treated by other new mothers as if her pregnancy and birth experience doesn't "count" because she doesn't have a baby to show for her efforts.
• fears that her child will reject her as not the "real" mother.	• fears that her child will grow up to hate her for her choice of making an adoption plan.
• (prior to placement) feels powerless and is terrified that she will say or do something to jeopardize the relationship.	• (after placement) feels powerless and is terrified that she will say or do something to jeopardize the relationship.
• struggles to talk to her child about his or her adoption.	• struggles to talk to her other (present or subsequent) child(ren) about their sibling's adoption.
• struggles to integrate her child's birth family into her own family identity.	• struggles to integrate her birthchild's family into her own family's identity.

When I first started working professionally in this field, I worked not only with birthmothers but also with prospective adoptive parents as well. My job was to complete a thorough evaluation called an "adoption home study." I was in my midtwenties, newly married, and had just started attending graduate school. In other words, I had been officially doing social work for about two and a half minutes! Many of the pre-adoptive couples I was assigned to work with were nearly twice my age, earned almost as much money in one month as I did in one year, and held degrees in subjects I knew absolutely nothing about. In those early days when I walked into a house to begin a home study, it wasn't hard to tell from the look on my new clients' faces that they were not entirely convinced that someone of my age and experience should be the one to decide whether or not they would make good parents. Despite the obvious differences, as soon as these sophisticated, driven professionals learned I was a birthmother, I had immediate credibility. It didn't take long for them to see that I understood what it meant to be in a place you never imagined yourself being, never wanted to be, and facing a road that you would rather not travel if given the choice.

Many times the families I met were totally against having any kind of openness in their adoption and espoused a litany of reasons for keeping their whereabouts a mystery from any birthmother. When I revealed that I was a birthmother, most people were fairly embarrassed because they could see I was a perfectly reasonable person, as well as a birthmother, and that there was nothing to fear. Many adoptive parents conveyed the same concerns like, "We are afraid our child will be confused by having two mothers" or "Doesn't visiting just make it harder for the birthmother to move on with her life?" When I was able to provide logical and reassuring explanations to their fears, most people were able to see the process as much less threatening and much more exciting.

Two Mothers?

All adopted children do have two mothers, a birthmother and an adoptive mother. One cannot replace the other. Nevertheless, your child will only have one mother who is the parent and provides for his day-to-day needs. There is no magic to genetics, and kids easily understand who is who. I always say, "Kids are only as confused as the adults around them."

There is common belief that successful grieving for birthmothers means arriving at a place in time when they have "moved on" with their lives, meaning they are able to pursue other interests without feeling the strong pull of missing their child. While this isn't completely untrue, a more accurate description of successful grieving would be "moving in"; in other words, achieving the integration of their child and their role as birthmother into her life. For a birthmother, visiting at any time in her child's life could trigger feelings of grief, but it will also provide proof of her child's well-being and solid reassurance that she made a good decision. Ultimately, this kind of "bittersweet" grieving will lead to her achieving a more full resolution of these losses than if she were to avoid seeing her child (and avoid the potentially painful reminders).

Many times I worried because an expectant mother I was working with appeared to have absolutely nothing in common with the family she had chosen. In one case, a birthmother considered a particular family because their profile included a picture of their dog, Sport, which looked just like the golden retriever she had when she was growing up. (Yes, you may agonize over creating the perfect profile, and it may just be your dog that actually is responsible for your adoption!) My worries proved unnecessary, time and time again. I witnessed unlikely unions form, as people who normally would not mix fell in love over a baby.

Success Story:
The Unlikely Match—Jimmy and Adette

ADETTE WAS A THIRTY-SEVEN-YEAR-OLD REGISTERED NURSE with a chatty personality and a huge smile. Her husband, Jimmy, a union ironworker, was a salt-of-the-earth, hardworking guy with a hard shell and a soft heart. Adette and Jimmy, together since the tenth grade, had already been married for nearly seventeen years when I was assigned to complete their home study. They had officially been trying to conceive since the very first day of their marriage, both eager to get started with duplicating the large, loud broods like the ones in which they had been raised. After years of nothing, followed by several more of fertility tests and treatments, Adette and Jimmy suffered the devastating loss of twins at seventeen weeks' gestation, just two weeks after Adette had finally felt safe enough to share the good news with their family.

After two years of grief and uncertainty, something happened that led Adette to believe that they were still meant to be parents, just not in the way they had originally thought. In a single day, Adette, a nurse in a pediatrician's office, had two new patients in a row. Both just happened to be newborn babies, and both just happened to be newly adopted. One adopted baby? Sure, that's a nice thing to hear about. Two adopted newborns? Probably a coincidence, but it definitely gave Adette a reason to pause. Before greeting her next appointment, Adette told God that if her next patient was another adopted baby, she would take that as a sign that they were supposed to adopt. What were the chances, anyway? She figured it was a pretty safe deal. (I'm guessing you don't need me to tell you what happened next!)

Jenny weighed about 100 pounds soaking wet and was already parenting a two-year-old son. She struggled to provide for him on her own while both working and going to school. When she found out that she was pregnant again, her boyfriend of three years moved out and she was truly alone. She saw Jimmy and Adette's advertisement, which said they wanted to adopt a baby, in the town's small local paper. She called them right away; that first conversation lasted more than an hour. They decided to meet in person to see if they wanted to pursue an adoption together.

Jimmy worried that Adette would get her hopes up for a baby and things wouldn't work out. What if Jenny didn't like them or decided to keep the baby? He was less than thrilled about driving three hours to meet this twenty-three-year-old pregnant woman in a small town in the middle of nowhere. He also knew that if he didn't, his wife would never speak to him again, so he dutifully went.

At their first meeting, Adette and Jenny talked about everything and anything, as if they were sisters. Even though Jenny was fourteen years younger than Adette, they did have a few things in common: they both had played on bowling leagues, enjoyed watching the same drama series on TV (don't tell me there aren't thousands of couples out there bonding over American Idol these days!), and Jenny was slowly working her way through school to become a nurse.

Jimmy didn't say much during the first meeting. He felt awkward and only asked Jenny if the baby was a boy or a girl. Jenny said she was sorry that she didn't know, and Jimmy assured her that it didn't matter; either a boy or a girl was great with him. (Jimmy told me that he always wanted a boy first, but I knew that a girl would be the biggest princess that ever lived if she became Jimmy's daughter.) It was only a few hours after they arrived home that they got a call from Jenny saying that she was "picking" them to be the adoptive parents and asked if they were okay with that or did they need more time to decide? Adette and Jimmy were more than excited, and after getting the necessary professionals involved, the official countdown to the birth began.

For the next ten weeks, Adette drove the three-hour stretch several times to see Jenny. Both Adette and Jimmy made the trip to witness Jenny's ultrasound. Jimmy and Adette had been through several miscarriages, two very late in Adette's pregnancies, so for them, ultrasound tests were also a reminder of the agonizing moments when they learned that their dreams of a baby were gone again. But Jenny's ultrasound appointment brought happy news: Jenny carried a healthy baby boy. Jimmy's eyes welled up with tears when the ultrasound technician told them the news.

After the appointment, Jimmy and Adette went with Jenny to pick up her son, Jared. They all went to McDonald's for lunch to celebrate, where Jared ate everyone's french fries. They took pictures of Jenny and Jared together. In one, Jared laid his head to the side, resting his cheek on Jenny's big round belly.

As the relationship of birthmother and adoptive parents solidified, Jenny asked Adette and Jimmy to be in the delivery room with her. Jimmy was more than a little anxious and shy about being there, but Jenny assured him that he could stand up by her head and he wouldn't see a thing.

Jenny's mother, Rhonda, who was the same age as Jimmy, was unsure about the "whole adoption thing," but told her daughter that she would support whatever decision she made. Rhonda was only seventeen years old when she gave birth to Jenny, and, as a single mom, she understood how hard it was to make ends meet and raise a child with no father present. She never had the chance to go to college, so she wanted Jenny to graduate. Jenny would be the first person in her whole extended family to earn a college degree.

Early on, we had recommended that Adette and Jimmy contract with a well-known licensed adoption agency located near Jenny's home, which would provide her with counseling services. This same agency also contacted the birthfather, inquired about his willingness to agree to the adoption, and since he was in agreement, offered for him to meet Adette and Jimmy. Fortunately, Dan, the birthfather, agreed to fill out the medical history form for the baby and sign whatever legal papers were needed from him. He was happy to read the adoption profile of Adette and Jimmy, but turned down the offer to meet them. He said that if Jenny liked them, that he was sure they must be good people. He was living about an hour away from Jenny and Jared and was employed as a mechanic and hoped to become a pilot one day. He had also recently found out that his new girlfriend was also expecting a baby, so, as he put it, his hands were full.

The local agency social worker also told him that Adette and Jimmy offered to send him regular updates on the baby's progress if he'd like. He declined this offer too, but he was happy to let her take his photo to give to the adopting parents. She gave him Adette and Jimmy's agency's information and told him that if he ever changed his mind and would like some photos or just wanted to know how his child was doing, the agency could act as an intermediary. He clearly stated that if his child ever needed anything medically, he would be fine with being contacted. Then he did what many birthfathers do; he chose to stay out of the picture.

Jenny cried when the social worker told her that Dan had signed the papers and was even quite polite. Since the lack of a stable relationship was one of the large factors for Jenny's decision to make an adoption plan, the reality that she not only faced the loss of her baby but also the loss of her first love suddenly became real to her. Like many other women I've known, Jenny secretly held on to the shred of hope that the baby she carried and shared with Dan would bring him back. In most cases, the birthfather doesn't show up to rescue mother and child, which often only adds to the devastating loss for the birthmother.

Delivery day came and Adette and Jimmy met Jenny at the hospital as planned. James Walter III was born on a blistering hot July day three days before his scheduled due date. After Jenny got an epidural, she and Jimmy played cards all afternoon. When it was time to push, Jimmy offered to leave the room, but Jenny insisted that he stay. Adette said he turned as white as a sheet, and she thought he was going to pass out, but he didn't. After sixteen hours of labor, James Walter III was born, and Jimmy cut the umbilical cord.

Speaking from experience, I know that the two days spent in

the hospital after giving birth feel like the longest days of your life. Time seems to stand still, while at the same time, it is over much too quickly. I distinctly remember that suddenly, after my son was born, the hue of the paint color on the walls changed a little, the sky had turned a slightly brighter shade of blue, and for some odd reason that no one could have explained to me before giving birth, I was seeing everything through a new lens. Ideas that seemed so simple before suddenly seemed complex and amazing. Other things that used to feel so important to me suddenly seemed trivial in light of the miracle of birth. The fact that I had created this perfect little person was both overwhelmingly beautiful and frightening at the same time. I was terrified that after this experience, nothing else in my life would ever matter as much or seem as significant as this baby did right then and there.

I don't know if this happens to adoptive mothers too, but I do know that I never had those exact feelings again—not even after giving birth to babies I knew I would parent. No one could have prepared me for that metamorphosis, although I wish someone had tried. This has always been my biggest challenge when counseling expectant mothers about adoption: how do you explain to someone what it is like to taste an entirely new and unfamiliar flavor or to see a new color for the very first time? After giving birth, woman after woman that I have counseled have said to me, "Ahhh . . . I didn't get it before, but now I know what you were saying."

I guess that is the miracle of motherhood. My big dilemma with this magical moment was that I was becoming a birth-mother, not a mother. And, sadly, that doesn't exempt women from still experiencing a seismic shift in their reality. I have the utmost respect for women who choose adoption for their babies after already being parents. To already know exactly how you are going to feel after your baby is born, but choose it anyways—now that is strength!

After little Jimmy was born, Jenny spent her time holding, feeding, and crying with him. Her mom visited and brought Jared to meet the baby. They took pictures of all of them together. Sometimes people forget that adoption often includes the loss of a sibling and grandchild too. I know this was hard for Jenny because she felt very protective of Jared. Her instinct as a mother was to protect him from any hurt he might feel later, realizing that he, too, lost a brother that day; but it made sense to her when her social worker explained that being open and honest with Jared from day one would make things much easier for him down the road.

As much as Jimmy and Adette loved Jenny, they still feared losing the baby. Even though Jenny joked with them to get some sleep (since it would be their last full night of it for a while), they couldn't. They paced, they stared at the television without watching, and they felt horribly conflicted because Jenny's heart was breaking. For many people, the emotional turmoil is the hardest part of this time. Adoption is full of conflicting emotions. The experience is bittersweet; it is happy-sad; your joy is someone else's pain.

It helped me a great deal to see my son being cared for by his new family. It assured me that I had made the right decision. It didn't make it comfortable, but at the same time, it did make it easier to see them so happy. It is a complete paradox: no one gains without first experiencing tremendous loss.

Jenny was a trooper. She never wavered from her plan. She signed the surrender papers after leaving the hospital and wrote a letter for little Jimmy to read someday. Even though Jenny, Adette, and Jimmy had planned to have contact after the birth, the bond of experiencing the birth together made that commitment even stronger. Jimmy, the muscle-bound, stoic ironworker said, "I never thought it could happen, but Jenny's in my heart. I can't imagine not seeing her again."

And they have. Not only do the visits they share two and

sometimes three times a year connect Jenny with her son, they also connect Jared with his brother and Jenny's mom with her grandson. They also reconnect Jenny with Adette and Jimmy. Their bond is strong and hopefully will last throughout little Jimmy's life. I know Adette and Jimmy worry that they will say something wrong or do something to make Jenny feel sad, as every adoptive family does, but I have reassured them that adorable pictures of Jimmy as a shy toddler clinging to his mommy's leg only confirms that Jenny got exactly what she wanted for her son. I hope that down the road the person who matters most in all of this will have the luxury of taking all of this for granted. James Walter III will never remember a time when he didn't know his birthmother, his birth grandmother, or his biological brother. To him, that will just be the way it's always been.

Adoption can be a beautiful, life-affirming process. Adoptive parents and birthmothers can experience the expanding and healing of their hearts through adoption, just as Jenny, Adette, and Jimmy did. And I will show you how.

4

Becoming Comfortable
with Being Uncomfortable:
Open Adoption

Sometime around my fourth month of pregnancy, I contacted what was then one of the most well-known and established adoption agencies in my area to set up an appointment. I attended a small, conservative liberal arts college located in a small, conservative—not much liberal or much arts—midwestern town. This agency aligned itself with much of the same belief system; definitely pro-life and definitely conservative. I went to the office located in the next town over because I didn't want to run the risk of seeing anyone even remotely associated with my college or, for that matter, my life. I would have been absolutely horrified if anyone had found out that I was pregnant.

Even though it was nearly twenty years ago, I still remember every second of my meeting at that agency. I remember the uncomfortable nuance of the quiet waiting room, the receptionist looking at me because I-knew-that-she-knew I was pregnant, and I remember the magazine on the coffee table with a large chubby baby on the cover. The social worker I met was a very plain-looking, middle-aged woman (okay, she was what I considered to be "middle-aged" then. I'm fairly certain I would describe her as someone much younger than middle-aged if we met today!), who was dressed in an extremely unremarkable gray cardigan sweater. Honestly, she looked exactly as I expected.

We got right to the issue at hand. I told her all of what I thought were the important parts of my situation; she asked me a few mundane questions, nothing surprising. Then I told her the one thing that I had decided I needed to go through with this adoption thing. I told her I wanted to meet the family I chose before I made a final decision.

Ms. Conservative Cardigan did not miss a beat. She told me, "Well, it really doesn't work that way, but what can happen is that after you have the baby and the papers are signed, you can meet the family here, at the office—without the baby, of course."

She continued, "You will arrive here first, then the family will come and you can spend a few minutes getting to know one another. Then the family will leave, and after that you can leave."

"So I have to just pick the family from a piece of paper?" I asked.

"Well, yes, all our families fill out a profile sheet for you to see, which includes all kinds of information about them."

"Does it have a picture of them?" I asked.

"No, but it has all their physical characteristics like height, weight, hair color, and eye color so you can choose someone who resembles you if you'd like."

"Okay, that's great, but don't you think that it is a little late for me to meet them after the adoption is already done? I mean, that kind of defeats the purpose of why I want to meet them to begin with."

My directness made this poor woman visibly uncomfortable.

"Well, yes, I'm sorry, but that is the way it works. There really is nothing different that I can do for you."

Suddenly, an enormous unspoken tension filled the room. I felt such shame, such embarrassment, and so pregnant and alone. My confident attitude dissolved. I suddenly felt like my bold attack of assertiveness had really been an irrational and unreasonable request. The harsh negative messages that I had learned so well as a child played over and over in my head. *I get it. I got myself into this predicament and I have no right to demand anything of the savior who is offering to help me out of it.*

At that moment I knew that I would never come back to that office again. Rather than tell the social worker, "This just isn't the right plan for me," I obediently made another appointment with the receptionist and pretended that everything was just fine, knowing that I would never walk into that office again.

Thank goodness for my good instincts. At the time I couldn't pinpoint the root of my discomfort, but later I came to realize I had received two unspoken, but nevertheless strong, messages that day. The first message was that birthmothers could not be trusted. Why did she want me to arrive at the agency before the adoptive parents? Probably so I would not see the car the adoptive family drove. The second message was that adoptive families need protection. The family would leave the office first—certainly to ensure that I could not follow them.

Why all the distrust? After all, wasn't I exactly the kind of woman who they would want to help? I was a twenty-one-year-old with strong ambitions and noble goals. I was taking good care of my unborn baby by seeing the doctor regularly. I didn't smoke or drink. I even went to church. After all, I chose life for my baby! If I wasn't trustworthy, what in the world did it take to meet that standard? I walked away from that agency feeling even more ashamed and afraid than before I had asked for help.

PEOPLE, LIKE TREES, HAVE ROOTS

When you consider the damage left in the wake of closed adoption, you can see why it quickly became a woman's last choice when faced with an unplanned pregnancy. This era of "We know better than you" social work unwittingly created a generation of angry and bitter birthmothers (and fathers), paranoid adoptive parents, and lost and disconnected adopted children who grew into adults with little, if any, knowledge about their ethnicity, medical history, or biological ties.

Thankfully, by the late 1990s, open adoption became the norm with laws still changing today as adopted children, birthmothers, and adoptive parents demand the rights that belong to them. Ironically, where I lived, one of the last-stand agencies to hold on to its closed-adoption ways happened to be the very same one I had first visited when planning my own adoption. When they did finally come around, they launched an enormous advertising campaign that claimed, "not only is open adoption the best thing to ever happen, what makes it even better is that we practically invented it!"—gag!

I was invited to speak on a panel of birthparents shortly after those billboards went up, and guess what agency just happened to be the sponsor? Okay, you guessed it: the same agency I had visited on that fateful day. Now guess which social worker was sitting in the audience. That's right, Ms. Gray Cardigan herself! I am still extremely proud of my self-control that day. Somehow I refrained from calling her out publicly, which was not easy, but instead I did my best to further my favorite cause—to support the rights of birthmothers—by just being the "you're-not-so-scary-after-all" birthmother panelist.

WHATEVER MAKES YOU COMFORTABLE

You will most likely hear the phrase "Whatever makes you comfortable" from some adoption professional, or you will read it in adoption marketing materials aimed at potential adoptive families. This phrase, in particular, represents one of my biggest pet peeves about the adoption industry. This is because adoption, by its very nature, is uncomfortable. What is comfortable about having a social worker come into your house and look into your closets? What is comfortable about handing over copies of your tax returns and disclosing any mistakes from your youth that may still be lurking around in your background check?

You'll also need to market yourself to complete strangers on the Internet—and this is all before you even get to the baby part! There are uncomfortable parts then, too, that take most new adoptive parents by surprise—like when you arrive home with your new baby and rather than feeling the expected joy and relief of a new parent, you feel guilty and grieved, as if you had stolen this baby rather than been given that beautiful gift that everyone talks about.

Birthmothers are often given the same sort of perimeters to operate within as well, when again, there is absolutely nothing comfortable about being faced with making what might just be the biggest decision of your life and is likely the hardest thing you will ever do. So it is of little comfort to most people when they are given two difficult options and told to choose the one that they are "most comfortable with." I have come to believe that the best approach I can advise you to take is to squarely face the reality that this process isn't going to be easy and comfortable, but that my job (or the job of the professional you may hire) is to give my clients as many tools and as much support as I can to help them make the very best choices for both themselves and their family.

One of the most widely used "Whatever makes you comfortable" statements is when it is used in relationship to how much contact or openness you would like in your adoption. Open adoption means different things to different people. Agencies define it differently; birthparents see it in one light and adoptive parents in another. In some states open adoption refers to a legal aspect of an adoption, while in other states it represents an informal agreement based solely on trust. Since open adoption can (and does) look so different depending on so many variables, let me first define what open adoption is *not.*

1. Open Adoption Isn't About You

Yes, sorry to say, this is true. But you know what? It isn't about me either. The open adoption process is geared to benefit the child first and foremost—not the adoptive parents or the birthmother. Now that my son Grey is older, I see the benefits of my difficult decision to participate in an open adoption. He knows who he looks like, he doesn't seem angry about being adopted, and he has no unanswered questions about his background or family history.

2. Open Adoption Is Not Co-Parenting

A birthmother (or first-mother, as some women prefer) gives life and then birth to a child. She provides her child with his or her biological history, race, and genetic links. The birthmother, not the adoptive parents, determines a child's left-handedness, eye color, and artistic talent. (The adoptive parents may be fully responsible for developing that artistic talent, but the seeds of creativity were planted long before by the birthmother and biological father.)

A parent is the person who is responsible for the day-to-day care and nurturing of a child. Parents have full legal rights to make decisions that affect that child and have full responsibility for the child's well-being.

In adoption, both the birthparent and the adoptive parents fulfill valuable, yet very different roles. The adoptive parents have no obligation to consult with their child's birthparent for input when making parenting decisions. Although a few states provide legal and enforceable open adoption agreements, these documents only address the kinds and amount of contact these families will have and do not allow anyone other than the adoptive parents to be responsible for making legal decisions regarding their child.

At one point in my son's life, his adoptive parents, Ron and Sybil, considered homeschooling him. They didn't solicit my opinion about homeschooling; the subject just happened to come up when we were talking one day. We had always been pretty honest with each other, and even though I don't remember my exact words, I do remember thinking it was a bad idea and feeling extremely anxious about it, so I'm fairly sure my initial response was probably pretty frank (and pretty negative!).

Even though Grey's parents decided not to homeschool him, it had nothing to do with me or my reaction. Regardless of what I felt, thought, or even knew to be fact, if Ron and Sybil had chosen to homeschool Grey, it was their decision to make. Having an open adoption did not mean that Ron and Sybil had to legally or morally ask my opinion or take my views into account at all when making this kind of decision. The birthparent gives up the right to make parenting decisions for her child as a result of the adoption.

However, because of my ongoing relationship with Grey's parents, I was able to tell them how I adapted to elementary school, which shed some light on how Grey might adapt. (As it turned out, my first-grade report card was practically identical to Grey's first-grade report card!)

Over our twenty-year journey together, there have been many decisions that Ron and Sibyl have made for Grey that I agreed with and many I didn't. I honored their decisions not only because legally I had no choice, but also—and more important—because I chose adoption for Grey so he would grow up in a strong and healthy family. Undermining those family relationships in any way would be counterproductive to that goal and certainly not aligned with what I chose for Grey. (Note that *choosing* is the operative word here. When birthmothers are forced to take the adoption route, they may not ever feel empowered in this way.)

Putting your child's needs before your own is a recurring theme for birthmothers in adoption. But let's face it—it's the same recurring theme for regular parents, too. Parents and birthmothers sacrifice for their children. As a birthmother, I was committed to making my relationship with Grey's parents work. At times this was hard for me, especially when I thought his parents made big mistakes and that I would have certainly done things differently! But I'll say it again: it isn't about me, it's about Grey, and Grey has a loving, stable, two-parent household. So it has always been worth it.

3. Open Adoption Is Not Measured by the Amount of Physical Contact

If we only view open adoption as a narrowly defined concept of visits—meaning physical contact with the birth family—then we discount an enormous number of children who have never had, and maybe never will have, any kind of direct contact at all. Many adoptive families feel that the amount and type of continued contact after placement is ultimately up to a birthparent's wishes (which, ironically, is exactly the opposite of what birthmothers usually believe!), and asking for more would be placing undue pressure on her. But whatever the reasons, the result of applying this strict definition is that many families would then, technically, have closed adoptions. So is it possible for a family who has no ongoing contact with any birth family (not by their own choosing, of course) to say that they still have an "open" adoption and be correct? I wholeheartedly say yes.

I once heard Sharon Kaplan Roszia, the coauthor of *The Open Adoption Experience,* say while speaking at an adoption conference, "If your door is open, you are practicing open adoption." What exactly does that mean? If you are an adoptive parent and are open to the possibility of your child one day developing a relationship with his birthparent, then you are implementing the principles behind open adoption as best you can. In other words, you leave the door open to foster a relationship in the future. The opportunity exists. In some cases, the birthparent lives far away or is not a safe person for your child to have contact with at the time, so as an adoptive parent, you may want to wait to pursue a relationship until later. Of course, if a birthparent is physically available and safe, then I encourage you to negotiate and facilitate an in-person relationship with the birthparent.

If a face-to-face relationship is not possible (one example may be if a birthparent is actively suffering from an addiction), I encourage you to foster an emotional relationship between your child and his birthparents. By explaining the concept of a birth family to your child in an age-appropriate way throughout his or her development, the child benefits by becoming secure with his whole identity, including his position within a birth family. In this emotional relationship, the adoptive parent considers the opportunity for the birthparent and child to meet should circumstances ever change. In other words, a child in this kind of adoption grows up always knowing about the birthparent and about the possibility of meeting one day.

Adoptive parents can foster a relationship with their child and his birthparents in many ways. The child may know her birthparent's name and that this person is her biological parent. A young child may know "I grew in her tummy," while an older child may know his birthmother chose not to parent him at the time because she was unmarried and felt strongly that he should grow up in a two-parent home. Often, there is a photo of the birthmother on display among other family pictures or on the nightstand next to the child's bed, conveying the message that this person holds a special place in the family's life. The adopted child may include her birthmother in nightly bedtime prayers or place an extra candle on each year's birthday cake as a way to acknowledge her significance on this day.

Maybe most important, the adoption comes up as a regular part of conversation with all members of the family contributing and commenting on the topic. The topic is not hidden or frowned upon; in fact, the adoption is just no big deal. When there are no secrets, there is no shame. Children are only as confused as the adults around them, and even when you don't have all the answers, letting a child explore, digest, and claim what is rightly theirs will go a long way in helping them make peace with their lives.

The less desirable alternative to this model is a family who has lots of openness with their child's birthmother, yet does not have the core values of an open adoption. At a recent birthmother retreat I facilitated, I met a young woman, Sarah, who was attending for the first time. After arriving at the retreat location, she realized that her drive home would take her right by where her son, Peter, lived with his adoptive family. She proceeded to give them a call (this was a Friday night) and ask if she could stop by to say hello on Sunday afternoon on her way home from the retreat. She excitedly shared her plan with the whole group during our Friday night tradition of each telling our adoption stories. She certainly described a thriving and healthy open adoption relationship with both Peter and his parents. In the eight years since Peter's birth, she enjoyed regular visits with him and his family and had developed a great relationship that included lightheartedness and joking, much like you would expect to see in extended family members.

Later in the weekend, Sarah revealed that her son did not even know he was adopted! She shared that his parents had recently told her they planned to tell Peter he was adopted by the year's end. Sarah raised the issue as a concern because she wondered if that also meant that Peter would be told she was his birthmother.

I was shocked by this revelation, because even though Sarah spent more time with her son than most of the women at the retreat, her relationship with him had been based on only half-truths. Although recognizing the awkwardness of the situation, Sarah genuinely believed she had a strong bond with her son and his family. She clearly had no idea how to deal with the implications of Peter finding out for the first time that she was not just "Sarah, friend of the family" but rather "Sarah, I grew in your tummy."

Ironically, this family seemed to be perfectly at ease with having their child's birthmother in their living room regularly. Instead of this causing them anxiety, what was apparently terribly hard for them was talking to Peter about his very own story. I have no idea what prompted the lack of disclosure. Maybe they had every intention of telling their son his story but when the time actually came, the words wouldn't come. Now, unfortunately for all of them, Peter may be the one who suffers from the secrecy and deception.

4. Open Adoption Is Not a Privilege; It Is a Responsibility

There are very few states with laws that address contact in adoption in any way at all, and even fewer where contact conditions apply to the adoption of a newborn. No state has laws that require adoptive parents to maintain contact with the birthparents and the child. So it's obvious that open adoption is not a right in any state. Anyone can enter into some type of open adoption agreement, whether it is written or simply understood. Most of the time the agreements are not legally binding or enforceable in any way, and they can never affect the legal status of an adoption.

Many agencies still use the idea of open adoption as a "carrot" to attract expectant mothers. They make carefully worded statements suggesting the expectant mother has clear choices or even "rights" regarding contact. Spence-Chapin, one of the oldest and most well-respected, not-for-profit adoption agencies in the United States, created a Birth Parent Bill of Rights that lists fourteen items introduced by, "If you are considering placing your baby in an adoptive home, you are entitled to certain rights, some of which are guaranteed to you by law." All fourteen items that follow are excellent ideas, and I agree that most are rights expectant mothers do have, although there are two statements that I feel are misleading: number 9 reads, "You have the right to choose ongoing communication with the adoptive family, including the exchange of pictures and letters," followed by number 10, "You have the right to choose open adoption. You and the adoptive family can choose to be in contact with each other through phone calls, letters, e-mails, and personal visits." Technically, these statements are true. Yes, a woman has the right to choose ongoing communication and open adoption. Yep, she has the right to choose—but that does not mean that she has the right to receive. Choosing and making it happen are two very different things.

Unless an expectant mother lives in one of the few states where the law provides for enforceable contact agreements (New York state, where Spence-Chapin is located, does not), contact is something she can request, hope for, even sign a written agreement with the adoptive family about, but she has no right and no way to ensure that this contact will ever occur. Yes, I do understand that agencies try to educate their families about the value of these relationships, and Spence-Chapin does a better job than many, but that still does not change the fact that most women who read this brochure will interpret post-placement contact as a right, only to find out that they have no rights at all.

Adoptive families obviously hold the legal power in an adoption, and even if they don't realize it, they hold the emotional power as well. I know many birthmothers who were promised a picture window into their child's life before placement, but after the papers were signed and everyone went home, they barely received a porthole. Every birthmother I have ever counseled has wondered if she could really trust the family she'd chosen. A birthmother wonders if the prospective parents weren't just telling her what she wanted to hear so they could get a baby. No doubt, these are legitimate fears, because some families agree to go along with open adoption because the agency may suggest that otherwise they would never be picked.

OPEN ADOPTION AS A PRIVILEGE

Having contact may not be a right, but some people may erroneously view it as a privilege. A privilege is something that one must earn, which also means it is something that can be taken away. A privilege is something not everyone gets, no matter how hard they try, and is defined as a "rare opportunity." When open adoption is viewed as a privilege, it exacerbates the already unequal power structure in adoption and makes a birthmother always dependent on an adoptive family's charity or goodwill. No matter how wonderful a birthmother acts (and maybe truly is), she will always worry that she has said or done something to warrant being "cut off" from her child. Many birthmothers feel they are always walking on eggshells around their children's adoptive parents, even years into the relationship. Living with this fear can stunt the growth of any authentic relationship and can prompt birthmothers to walk away when it becomes too stressful and difficult.

I remember my palatable exhale of relief when Grey became old enough to have a voice in our relationship. Sometime around age nine, his adoptive mom called to relay a direct request from Grey that I come visit soon. I finally felt that unless I did something completely awful (which I'm not even sure what that would've been), Grey would still want to see me, and his parents would have a much harder time denying our relationship. I know my anxiety over the years was unfounded. I have talked to Ron and Sybil about these feelings, and they were shocked! Never in Grey's life had they ever even considered severing my contact with Grey. They had no idea I ever worried and said that if they had known, they would have tried harder to reassure me. I'm not sure that would have made one bit of difference, but it was nice to hear that they felt that way.

Some birthmothers initially will not want contact because they fear that seeing their child will be too painful for them. If they are trying very hard to remain emotionally unattached to their baby in order to protect themselves, this would make perfect sense.

An expectant mother who is already parenting children is faced with additional challenges. Chapter 20 is entirely dedicated to the subject of siblings, because they impact many parts of an adoption. The mother must make decisions not only for the child she is expecting but also for the ones she is already parenting.

Lots of families have asked me, "Wouldn't it be easy to convince a birthmother to stay involved, since it seems like after the baby is born, she always wants more contact than she thought?" It would seem so, and right after her baby is born, pretty much every new birthmother can't imagine a day when she would not want to stay involved in an open adoption. After a birthmother first says good-bye to her new baby and then grieves so deeply, she thinks of her child all the time. As that initial, intense grief begins to subside, she thinks of her baby less; eventually she may go a whole day, or two, or even three without thinking much about the adoption. Then at that point, a visit with her child can reopen the wound of longing, and if there is no one to support her in her grief after those visits, she will likely back off from contact to avoid the pain.

Other books on adoption (not written by birthmothers) will tell you the birthmother may "move on with her life" and will need less contact. In truth, what she needs is some support to help her stick with the visits, even though they are painful. But it's not uncommon that birthmothers often don't get the support they need, so they may walk away from the relationship, sadly, primarily out of self-preservation.

Several years ago, I ran into a family whose daughter's birthmother I had counseled during their adoption. They told me how at first they sent photos and always got a note in return. They saw her a few times that first year too, but as the months passed, they continued to send letters but received no response from the birthmother. They tried calling too, but the number was disconnected. Because the parents became so discouraged, they wrote a letter to the birthmother and said if they did not hear from her soon, they would assume she did not want any further contact, and they would stop sending updates.

I do not know why their daughter's birthmother stopped answering their letters, but I can speculate that she would not respond to their ultimatum either. If she didn't know what to say before, she certainly wouldn't know what to say now.

I challenged this adoptive mom on her presumption that this young woman's silence meant she no longer wanted updates on her daughter. I asked her simply, "Instead, why didn't you write that if she does not want any more contact to let you know, so you can respect her wishes, but until then, you would just assume her silence meant she did want updates and you would continue to send photos?" This mom looked surprised by my suggestion and said, "Oh, gee, I never even thought of that."

OPEN ADOPTION AS A RESPONSIBILITY

When I present open adoption as a responsibility to birthmothers, I counsel them that the minimum contribution to an open adoption is for them to send an annual update, telling their child's family where they are and how they are. Often I am the only person giving birthparents advice about maintaining contact with their children. By nature, the adoption "setup" tends to communicate just the opposite.

If this same adoptive family approached this relationship from a responsibility point of view, they, too, could have continued sending updates to their daughter's birthmother (regardless of whether or not they received a response) and they could also keep a copy of everything they ever sent, for their child to have someday. This "keep a copy" method also works well in situations where the adoptive family loses track of their child's birthmother. Keeping a copy of everything will show your child that you always valued their birthmother. If the birthmother no longer has a valid address, the adoptive family can send letters and photos to their agency or attorney, or perhaps another birth relative or mutual friend, to hold for safekeeping. In this case, if the birthmother does resurface, she would immediately know the family valued her, which would help make her more at ease about reestablishing some kind of communication.

Taking these steps will help reinforce your child's self-worth by showing them that biological ties are sacred and should be valued. Whatever the case, there are always things that you can do to ensure that your child will someday know that you always valued these biological ties and made the effort to ensure their survival. Your efforts will show your child that you consider them to be worthwhile.

Clearly, open adoption contact can help build lasting, loving relationships with your child and the adoptive parents. It is by far the best approach for a lifetime of happiness, growth, and satisfaction for the child, parents, and birthparents involved in the adoption.

In twenty years, I predict (or at least I hope) children and their birthmothers will come out of the closet. Birthmothers won't be shrouded in secrecy. Children will refer to their birthmothers as comfortably as they make reference to aunts and uncles. You can define family as broadly or as narrowly as you choose, and extended families add love and blessings to our children's lives. Let birthmothers give the gift of love to their children. The more a child is loved, the more the child will benefit and be able to give love in return.

5

Why "Agency" Can Be a Four-letter Word

My recommendations for a successful and rewarding adoption vary greatly from the usual practices employed by most agencies. Before I start outlining my process, I'd like you to know my reasoning behind it. I want you to understand why this process works better than most and how you can benefit from my experience.

Based on my approach, you may mistakenly assume that I am anti-agency or that I am discouraging you from using the services of an agency. Nothing could be further from the truth. Many excellent agencies exist and their expertise and experience can prove invaluable. On the other hand, there are some unscrupulous agencies that do not have everyone's best interests at heart. I am advocating that you make an informed decision about when and for what specific purpose you enlist the services of an agency in your adoption, and if you do, how to find the very best one.

KNOW THE FACTS

To successfully manage your own adoption process, you need to educate yourself first. The more you know, the more confident and in control you will feel and the less anxiety you are likely to experience. Some agencies have a "we know better than you" approach to the process, which can cause you to feel anger and resentment toward the people who are supposed to be your allies. I have watched families go through the entire adoption process biting their tongues because they felt they had no choice but to agree with the policies or practices of a dictatorial agency in order to have a family. Families who have suffered with infertility struggles and unsuccessful treatments may find the adoption route equally as frustrating.

Through my approach, you can avoid needing to fit a profile for acceptance into a traditional agency, where you can run the risk of rejection. If you are too old, too young, your spouse practices a different religion, you practice no religion, you have a chronic or previous health issue, you have other children by birth, you have other children by adoption, you're single, you're gay, whatever your circumstances, your options may appear extremely limited when it comes to your choice of agencies. A state's requirements for who is allowed to adopt a child are generally quite broad and less strict than ones imposed by an agency. (You can begin by investigating your state's general requirements, and then you can compare them to any agencies' requirements. Most state government websites contain a section about adoption that answers these questions. Look for something like, "Who can adopt?" or "Who is allowed to adopt a child?" and you will likely find these answers listed there.) Because the number of families hoping to adopt each year far outweigh the number of women making adoption plans for their babies, agencies can establish very particular requirements for acceptance that extend beyond what any state law requires. Depending on where you live and what your budget looks like, you may have already lost hope to adopt. Don't despair. I'm here to renew that hope and help you find the answers and give you the tools to succeed with an adoption.

I firmly believe that there is an ideal adoption match for everyone. Many birthmothers I know chose their adoptive families for the very reasons those families may have been rejected from agencies. For example, Elise placed her son with Susan and Jim, who didn't meet and fall in love until each was more than forty years old. By the time they found their way to adoption, they were too old (in their early fifties) for most agencies to accept them. Their ages were not a negative issue to Elise since they had active lifestyles and healthy habits. Elise recognized they were in far better shape than her own parents, who were much younger. Ironically, while Susan and Jim worried their ages put them at a disadvantage, Elise loved the idea that they were established, mature, and ready to become parents.

In another example, Dan and Amanda both suffered from type 1 diabetes. Amanda's doctor said that because of her condition, it would be unwise for her to get pregnant. So the couple decided to adopt, but were told by various agencies that an expectant mother would not select them if they shared information about their health problems. Both Dan and Amanda felt that not being up front about both of them being diabetic would be unethical. They believed any woman who would trust them with her child had a right to know the truth. As Dan said, "If we are asked why we're adopting, we would be faced with, at the very minimum, telling a half-truth, if not a bold-faced lie." They openly shared their reasons for pursuing adoption with every expectant mother, and some did reject them. But when they found Julie, they knew they had made the right decision. Julie's mother was also a diabetic, and as a single parent, her mom had always made sure that she took care of herself physically. Living with a chronic health condition was a normal part of life for Julie's mom, so she didn't see it as a deal-breaker. She looked at the situation pragmatically; any family could develop a health condition in the future (maybe even something much worse!). There are no guarantees.

Valerie, another client, chose Frank and Kathy as the adoptive parents for her child when she learned that Frank was a recovered alcoholic who now helped others with their sobriety. Alcoholism was a disease that ran in her own family, and knowing that Frank and Kathy had experience with it was a huge relief to Valerie.

Candy and Rick are an example of a birthmother and birthfather who, planning together, chose a single woman named Roberta to adopt their daughter, even though they had considered many married couples. In their opinion, having a mom and a dad alone did not ensure that a family was stable or happy. They both felt strongly that Roberta's close-knit family and strong network of friends would help her provide a better home than either of them had experienced coming from two-parent households. Initially they were drawn to Roberta by her letter, which conveyed her sense of humor. After meeting her in person, they established a strong connection.

Time after time, I have experienced the joy of seeing families who would have been turned away from agencies, for a variety of reasons, become the perfect family for an expectant mother. A gay-rights activist, Margot specifically searched for only lesbian couples so her daughter would be raised in an accepting environment. Maggie chose adoptive parents already parenting three biological sons—she loved the idea that her daughter would have three older brothers to protect her. Adrian chose an adoptive mother for her son who was infertile as a result of cancer treatments. Her own mother had successfully battled the same cancer and Adrian was outraged that suffering from cancer could prevent someone from being able to adopt a baby. Often, just seeing that an adoptive couple is not perfect—that they have the same struggles and problems we all do—can affirm a women's choice to pick them.

For all of these families, the things a traditional agency would consider a disadvantage became the very things that helped attract their children's expectant mothers to them. By being honest, these families found the children they were meant to have, and that meant that they, too, would be someone's perfect family.

THE MATTER OF TRUST

I never advocate withholding significant information from an expectant mother. Don't be surprised if some adoption "professionals" tell you that this is a perfectly acceptable thing to do. Yes, disclosure does mean you are taking the risk that some expectant mothers will walk away, but here is another valuable aspect you may not have thought of: by sharing tough information with the person who is considering entrusting you with her most valuable achievement—her baby—you are immediately demonstrating honesty and integrity, two qualities that will go a long way to helping the birthmother gain enough confidence to follow through with her adoption plan with you. In every single adoption I've ever seen, after the baby is born, the new mother, sitting in her hospital bed and holding her tiny baby, looks over to me and asks how she can really know that she can trust these people with her baby. There is nothing I or any other social worker can do to convince her to trust you—you need to be the one to cultivate and grow that trust.

WHY PAYING AN AGENCY
DOESN'T ALWAYS PAY OFF

My adoption process works because it is simple by its very nature, and somewhat self-selecting. I offer an empowering plan where an expectant mother contacts a family directly. By doing so, they are already at an advantage in several ways.

1. This expectant mother is farther down the road in her decision-making process.

Many agencies offer "pregnancy counseling," or help the expectant mother decide whether she should parent or make an adoption plan. She is often in the early months of pregnancy, scared, and looking for help. Of course, I do think this is a much-needed and valuable service, but it generally appeals to the expectant mother who is still unsure about what her plan will be.

A woman who calls a family directly has already made the decision to carry her pregnancy to term, decided that adoption is her primary plan, and begun searching for a family. She may have decided on adoption months ago, before getting the courage to actually move forward with her plan (which in many cases is helpful, since she has had some time to let it "percolate"). This does not mean that a woman who fits this profile will never vacillate between parenting and adoption, which is normal and even encouraged, but it does mean the expectant mother has already come far in her emotional decision to move forward with the adoption.

2. An expectant mother who calls a family directly chose not to call an agency.

From my experience, many expectant mothers are put off by the concept of working with an agency. I regularly trained families who were looking to adopt to use words other than "agency" to describe the help they received with their adoption. If the birthmother had wanted to connect with an agency, she would've opened the phone book and called one. Because she didn't, she was obviously looking for a more direct approach, one that took out the middle man. This doesn't mean that an agency can't play a useful role in your placement, but realize that some expectant moms hear the word "agency" and think "big, hierarchical (and often religious) organization who is going to butt in and tell me what to do."

Eventually, I let all my clients know that at one point I did work for an actual adoption agency, but I wait to share this until after they have connected with the family directly. I then begin to counsel the expectant mom on the specifics of the process, as well as her rights and choices. I know that many of these women based their assumptions about agencies on their own past negative interactions with

various social service organizations or on what they had heard. I
didn't want to alienate them from the get-go with this information.
I know their reaction to meeting with me at the start would have
been much more hesitant and skeptical if they knew I had agency
experience.

3. An expectant mother who calls a family directly is taking an active role in moving her adoption plan forward.

I am sure the prospect of taking a call from an expectant mother
directly is unnerving. Well, that is exactly what it is like for the
expectant mother on the other end of the line as well. To pick up
the phone and call a complete stranger about something as intimate
as adoption takes significant courage. In fact, let's face it—the birthmother's got some guts!

This kind of proactive step is quite telling in many ways. It means
the birthmother is capable of taking steps forward toward a goal. I
believe this is the exact reason this method of adoption has fewer
"fall-throughs" than a traditional agency adoption. The type of person who is willing to pick up the phone to begin with is also the
type of person who is much more likely to follow through with an
adoption plan.

I used this approach in my own adoption. Remember, I visited an
agency, had a negative experience there, and then went on to find a
family on my own. I am quite certain that had I not taken this
approach and had continued with an agency, I would be the parent
of an adult son right now! It was my direct interaction and relationship with Grey's parents and my ability to shape the placement (in
the few ways I could) that gave me the strength to complete my
plan. If I had to pick just one thing that was most significant in
helping me stick with the adoption plan, it was the fact that I knew
and loved Ron and Sybil and felt in my heart that we were all on the
same team.

TEAM EFFORT

I have seen traditional agency adoptions where the standard of "good practice" is one that basically pits adoptive parents and birthparents against one another. They use words like "negotiation" and "mediation," which immediately infers an upcoming adversarial process. It is hard to get the impression that everyone is on one team if the first interaction an expectant mother has with the family she has chosen involves meeting across an agency conference room table with both sides' social workers present and no last names provided (the birthmother may never learn the adoptive parent's last name).

I do believe that the ethical practice of adoption is possible without creating a system of "them" and "us." It is possible to ensure that everyone's rights are respected and needs are met in a legally sound way, while at the same time creating a strong foundation on which to build the rest of this child's life in an open adoption. I feel strongly that every expectant mother should receive counseling in every adoption, both before and after placement (especially if a licensed adoption agency is not involved in the placement) from someone specifically trained in adoption practice. The counselor or social worker should operate on the premise that an expectant mother is just that—an expectant mother—and always retains the right to parent her child until she signs legal documents. (Without that premise, counseling can easily become coercion!) Yet if we are mapping out lifelong relationships here, I just don't think that an orchestrated division is the most helpful way to begin. I talk to birthmothers every day who are struggling with some issue related to this complicated relationship between birth and adoptive family, and feel angry and resentful toward an agency that did not provide them with the tools they would need after the agency was long gone.

IF SHE'S SO GREAT,
WHY DOESN'T SHE JUST PARENT?

I've pointed out many advantages to this approach to adoption, but there is still one obvious disadvantage that often troubles adoptive parents in more ways than one: the same qualities that are such strong predictors of a successful adoption are also the same qualities that would make this expectant mother a great parent.

There are two ways that this often comes up in an adoptive family's thoughts. First is the situation that I, myself, fell into. I could have parented. I not only had the resources available to me, I had significant people in my life pressuring me to not make an adoption plan for Grey. My reasons for choosing adoption were more related to my not being ready to parent and knowing that this was not in the best interest of my son than because I didn't have the financial or emotional support. This isn't always true, but when it is, it makes the waiting even more nerve-racking for the adoptive parents because the birthmother could change her mind at any time, with few hurdles to overcome in order to provide for that baby.

Because the birthmother may have the resources to parent, the adoptive parents might actually find themselves feeling guilty about depriving the birthmother of that opportunity. Many adoptive mothers have told me that there was at least one time along the way when they wanted to throw their arms around this woman and do whatever they could to persuade her to parent! The emotional maturity needed to understand that even though you *could* parent doesn't mean you *should* is exactly what causes conflicted feelings and sometimes even guilt. (This point illustrates the need for a process called "entitlement," which I will talk more about in Chapter 18.)

If I had decided to parent Grey after all, as painful as it would've been for Ron and Sybil, I know they would've been okay. Yes, even though they would've suffered a tremendous loss, I'm sure they would've even wished me well. They would've known Grey would have a good life, and then I believe they would've gone on to adopt successfully. Even when you believe that we all get the children we are meant to have, it is still heartbreaking to hear adoptive mothers say that, years later, they still pray for that baby—who was not meant for them to adopt—to have a good life.

Part II
"Simple Reproduction" Is an Oxymoron

6

The Many Roads to Adoption

There are multiple avenues all leading to the same destination when traveling in the land of domestic infant adoption. It helps me to think of the adoption process as dining in a restaurant with an à la carte menu. Maybe this metaphor will help you, too.

In my restaurant, à la carte means everything is separate and you pick from many foods and the number of courses you want. This means that your meal could end up being quite different from the one being served at the next table. The basic concept of food and satisfying one's hunger is the one common theme for everyone in my restaurant, but the different choices available ensure that each person's dining experience will end up varying, at least to some degree.

Just like at any restaurant, at mine there are always some limitations that will impact your selections, such as what foods are available and how much money you can afford to spend. Some people in my restaurant choose one item from each course, while others have one course instead of two; for example, rather than having an appetizer and a salad, they simply order a dinner-size salad.

At my restaurant, everyone is required to order an entrée, and often dessert is included. (I wouldn't go so far as to say that dessert is free, but rather its cost is built-in to the price of the entrée, making it seem more economical.) Depending on the food you receive and the quality of service, you may leave feeling extremely satisfied and look forward to your next dinner at the same restaurant. Undoubtedly, some people will wish they could've had just one more course or that their server was more efficient. Or maybe they wished they were given a more accurate description of their dishes before they ordered them and a better estimate of length of time their food would take to reach the table. Regardless, everyone at my restaurant pays for what they get, but unfortunately, not everyone will feel they got what they paid for.

Adoption agencies and organizations, like restaurants, vary in the service and food they provide. Thai food is quite different from French, yet they both accomplish the same goal—satisfying your hunger through different tastes and experiences.

THE PRIVATE AGENCY

Private agencies operate independently under a license issued by the state in which they are located. Every state dictates its own standards for licensing, and in some states adoption agencies are licensed as a "child placing agency," while in others they may be called a "child welfare agency." Some states do not require that a licensed agency maintain a staffed office in that state; some may not even require that the agency have a physical location at all. A private agency may be either for-profit or not-for-profit. Some states require that all adoption agencies be not-for-profit entities, while in others they may be either.

Forget, for a moment, how the words "for-profit" sound when placed before the words "adoption agency," and consider instead that the primary difference between these two types of agencies is not in the actual adoption services they provide, but rather in the way they conduct business and have set up the structure of their organization.

Not-for-profit agencies are referred to as a "501C-3," which indicates the IRS code that governs the tax-exempt status they enjoy. They may or may not be affiliated with a particular religious organization. Not-for-profit agencies are required to have a board of directors, must publish an annual financial report, and must reinvest a certain amount of profit back into the organization as per IRS rules. For-profit agencies are not required to have a board of directors, nor are they required to make their financial information public. They may take whatever percentage of profits home in their pockets just as any other business entrepreneur would and are also subject to all of the same federal taxes and fees as with any small business.

So what does that all mean? It means you will still find highly paid directors at a not-for-profit agency, and you may discover the fees they charge are no less than what the general market can bear. The inverse can also be true. You can certainly find a for-profit agency with modestly paid employees, frugal spending, and competitive fees. There were several times during my ten years with a for-profit agency that the two founding directors did not bring home paychecks during the lean times.

A licensed private agency is allowed to complete home studies and, per state law, complete final surrender papers or relinquishments (the legal documents that when filed in court will terminate parental rights over a child) from expectant mothers following birth. They can compile and complete interstate compact adoptions (meaning that the state in which the baby is born or the birthmother resides is different from your state of residence and requires additional paperwork), and, in some states, file court documents on your behalf.

Some licensed private agencies offer programs in more than one kind of adoption. They may have a program that finds homes for older children currently in the foster care system or for children with special medical needs. They may offer international adoption home studies or even have their own programs in foreign countries. Some agencies have different types of programs within the domestic infant adoption process to choose from. They may offer a more traditional approach to adoption that includes submitting a profile letter and then simply waiting in a pool to be chosen by an expectant mother who comes to the agency or the other extreme where you are fully responsible for finding any potential birthmother with your own marketing efforts. Between these two extremes, some agencies will also offer à la carte services to assist with a domestic adoption, allowing you to choose some particular services without ordering everything on the menu.

THE ADOPTION FACILITATOR

Adoption facilitators are unlicensed and largely unregulated individuals whose primary goal is to connect prospective adoptive parents with expectant mothers for a fee. Very often, facilitators are not formally educated in either social work or law. Rather, they are simply individuals passionate about adoption, often having adopted children themselves. They may have backgrounds in sales or marketing.

State laws range from prohibiting the adoption facilitator practice, to regulating it through the use of a formal registration process, to no regulation at all. You may also see facilitators referred to as adoption intermediaries, advertising specialists, brokers, adoption advocates, or matching agents. Regardless of the name, they all provide the same service for a fee.

Facilitators generally operate in one of two ways. One is to create a network of contacts, including agency workers, attorneys, clergy, or other individuals who may encounter pregnant women who are considering adoption. There may or may not be a financial incentive for these contacts to provide a referral to a particular facilitator. The facilitator then either contacts a family that has already paid them a fee and are waiting for their "match," or if the facilitator does not have an appropriate family for the client, they may initiate contact with multiple licensed agencies (usually via mass e-mail), asking if they have any prospective adoptive families who might be interested. The prospective adoptive couple must then pay the facilitator's required fee for the "match."

Facilitators may also purchase advertising on the Internet, in telephone books, and in newspapers by pooling together all the fees they collect. Their advertising usually includes a toll-free number that gives no indication of a location or identity of the service, but usually employs a teaser line like "all expenses paid." The facilitator then fields all the calls generated by the advertising and matches the expectant mother with a prospective family. How this match is done varies from facilitator to facilitator.

It is important that you check the laws of the state in which you live, as well as the state where the facilitator is located, and where the birth of the baby you hope to adopt will occur. All of these state laws have the potential to impact your adoption when paying fees for a "match." Most likely, all monies you have paid out in an adoption will need to be reported to the court where your adoption is filed, and if paying a facilitator is not legal in your jurisdiction, you may encounter a problem.

One disturbing practice among a few licensed agencies is that they now function in much the same way that a facilitator does, meaning they demand large fees for leads on possible adoption situations generated by their own advertising efforts. Whenever I was working with an expectant mother, and for whatever reason, if our agency did not have the right family for her, it was common practice to network among other agencies to locate one who did. Then the other agency would send us their client's home study and profile (a topic we will cover thoroughly in Chapters 7–9) to present to the expectant mother. If the mother chose that family, we would work together in an arrangement called an "interagency placement" to complete the plan.

Be aware: there are some agencies (who must spend enormous amounts of money on advertising) who field calls from expectant mothers all over the United States and establish an initial rapport with these women via the telephone. Given how anxious most expectant mothers are at that point, she may find a sympathetic ear and someone who promises help on the line, so she may not call another (perhaps local) agency and receive counsel in person.

In the case that the advertising agency doesn't have any appropriate waiting families to send, they will compile some basic information about the expectant mom's situation, along with what type of adoptive family she is looking for, and e-mail it to a huge number of agencies. Some organizations will send out a single e-mail soliciting for more than one situation at once. I have seen information for as many as twelve expectant mothers in one e-mail. The e-mails reveal the state where the expectant mother lives, when she is due, any special needs known, and always includes the financial arrangement for living expenses promised to the mother prior to the birth.

At one point, I was working with a family seeking a birthmother and received an e-mail about an expectant mother who wanted a family with the characteristics that mine possessed. When I contacted the agency sending the e-mail, they agreed that my waiting family really did sound like the perfect match. The shocking news was the agency expected my family to pay a $14,000 matching fee for the lead alone! Keep in mind that the $14,000 fee did not go to the expectant mother or provide for her, it simply paid the agency for the "match." Clearly, this licensed agency was working with its own best interests in mind, not the child's or the mother's.

THE ADOPTION ATTORNEY

The terms "independent adoption" or "private adoption" describe an adoption in which an attorney facilitates the bulk of the process with little involvement from a social worker. These adoptions still require a home study prior to an adoptive placement (except in some very rare cases), and a number of visits by a social worker or licensed agency representative after placement but prior to an adoption becoming finalized.

An adoption attorney's role in the adoption process varies widely from state to state. For example, in Indiana an attorney is not prohibited from advertising on behalf of adopting couples, customarily meets and assists expectant parents with pre-placement paperwork (note that I did not call this "counseling," even though this may be the only counsel she receives), physically goes to the hospital and completes legal consents with the birthmother (consents are the documents a birthparent signs to voluntarily relinquish her parental rights), and later files them in court on the family's behalf. This same law office may also function as an intermediary later for letters and pictures sent back and forth between the birth and adoptive families. In a state where an attorney is not legally allowed to complete all of these functions, obviously, this type of "attorney-only private adoption" would not be possible.

In contrast, in my home state of Michigan, neither adopting nor birth families are required to have representation by an attorney; rather, agencies routinely complete the necessary legal documents, including the adoption petition, and file them in the court of proper jurisdiction directly on their client's behalf. Attorneys in Michigan rarely play a role in routine adoptions. My attorney friend in another state often teased me that I was practicing law without a license; nevertheless, it was all perfectly legal here. Be aware that you would not have to travel very far for that to not be the case!

Given that adoption is a multifaceted issue, every placement usually has several social, emotional, medical, ethical, and last, but definitely not least, legal issues. Technically, you could ignore all but one of these issues—the legal requirements. While legal issues are a critical component of the adoption issue—I don't recommend you ask Uncle Frank, a real estate attorney, to do your adoption for you—don't forget about all the other issues that come into play. A lawyer can only assist with the legal aspects of the adoption, not the social, emotional, or medical issues that come into play.

The only advice my attorney gave me was to "Call me when the baby's born." I received no counseling. None. Ron and Sybil received no counseling; they didn't even complete a home study until after we had gone to court and I had permanently relinquished my parental rights. Legally, I had no idea how the process was going to work; I just trusted that since our attorney said it would work, it would. He did a great job with what he was trained to do, and even though I wish someone would have suggested it, I don't blame him for not persuading me to talk to someone about it.

Many attorneys do offer counseling referrals to their adoption clients; either they contract with a local licensed social worker, or, less often, they have a counselor on staff. What I have heard most from attorneys who offer these optional services is that most women just aren't interested. Unfortunately, the idea of seeing a "therapist" or "getting counseling" still carries a stigma for some people. When an attorney asks an expectant mother, "Would you like counseling?" most often her immediate response is "no," with the thought, *I'm not crazy; are you saying that there's something wrong with me?*

Law school teaches pragmatic thinking, so it isn't surprising that attorneys don't realize that if they were to relabel the counseling process, using a word like "advocate" rather than "counselor," it would be far more likely that women would accept their offer. Also, lawyers should refer to the service as a routine part of every adoption rather than an optional service.

OTHER ADOPTION PROFESSIONALS

When you begin to investigate adoption, you will quickly realize the term "adoption professional" can mean any number of things, including social worker, psychologist, or a therapist. In these cases, the adoption professional has a formal education in that field and probably holds some type of professional license. For example, many states require that in order to be in a supervisory position within a child welfare organization (the umbrella under which most adoption agencies fall), you must have a particular degree and/or professional license; for example, one might need to be a licensed clinical social worker. In contrast, anyone wanting to informally help put together adoptive placements might call themselves a facilitator, matching agent, advisor, advocate, consultant, or any other title they would like to give themselves. Remember that in most states these kinds of "professionals" are largely unlicensed and unregulated, so one should not assume that someone with "Dr." in front of his or her name holds a degree that has anything to do with children whatsoever. If the organization you are talking to is anything other than a licensed agency or an attorney, make sure to ask questions about the person's education as well as experience.

Most often these professionals function simply by helping pregnant women or already born babies find waiting families. Depending on the state, an adoption professional may function in a way similar to a facilitator but legally cannot (or simply do not) charge fees. Sometimes affiliated with a religious organization, they see adoption as a worthy cause, whether because they adopted a child themselves and would like to help others adopt, or because they want to offer assistance to women in crisis pregnancies. Whatever their motivation, it is your responsibility to ask the adoption professional for detailed information about their background, experience, role, and motivation.

Gay and Lesbian Adoption

Domestic adoption by gay and lesbian couples is becoming more commonplace than ever before. In September 2008, the Evan B. Donaldson Adoption Institute released a "Policy and Practice Prospective," looking at the current practices in adoption, examining the most current scientific evidence available, and, based on this, issuing recommendations in support of gay and lesbian families.

Studies reflecting twenty-five years of social outcomes show that, in general, children raised in nontraditional households fare just as well as children raised by heterosexual parents. Thirteen of the leading organizations representing children's best interests, including the American Academy of Pediatrics and the American Academy of Child and Adolescent Psychiatry, have issued formal statements in favor of allowing gay and lesbian families to adopt. (A complete list of these organizations can be found at the back of this book.) This issue has been addressed primarily from the practice of nontraditional families adopting children from state foster care systems, but for all practical purposes, the legal allowances (or restrictions) can be applied in the same way, whether you are hoping to adopt a six-year-old or a six-week-old child.

Currently, adoption by a gay or lesbian individual is prohibited, by statute, only in the state of Florida. Two other states, Utah and Mississippi, specifically prohibit gay couples from adopting. (Utah prohibits any unmarried, cohabiting couple from adopting regardless of their sexual orientation.) In many other states, same-sex couples are allowed to adopt jointly, either at the same time referred to as a "second parent adoption" or "co-adoption," making both partners legal parents of the child.

In theory, co-adoption could occur in all of the forty-seven remaining states, but I say "in theory" because technically, although these states' statutes do not *prohibit* this practice, they do not *provide* for it specifically either. So in other words, where joint adoption is accepted, it is not because of what state's statute specifically says, but rather because of what it doesn't say.

Obviously, this practice could always be opened to further interpretation by the courts at any time (and often is). To complicate things further, there are many states in which adoption by gay and lesbian couples is routine in some jurisdictions but completely unheard of in another right down the road.

Even if you are residents of a state that specifically prohibits you and your partner from adopting together (or it just isn't done), it may still be possible for you to complete a second parent adoption in another state if the child is born there. But, as you may already well know, you might then have problems getting a second parent adoption recognized in your state of residence.

The best way to find out if the state in which you hope to adopt from is "adoption friendly" to you is to contact an attorney who is a member of the American Academy of Adoption Attorneys and seek specific advice (www.adoptionattorneys.org).

7

A Great Excuse to Clean
Your Closets: The Home Study

Now that you understand the different kinds of adoption resources out there, you might be surprised to learn that much of what all those resources offer in terms of services are things that you can actually learn to do on your own. If you are someone who likes to take charge, be in control of your own destiny, and save a ton of money at the same time, then this is where my book will begin to get exciting for you! I promise that there are pieces and parts of your adoption that you can do yourself (which will still save you time and money), but you can still hire a professional for the rest. Knowing what you can and can't (or don't want to) do is more than half the battle.

If you are a nontraditional family (meaning single, gay, or lesbian), the home study process I describe here should be primarily the same process any family will experience, with a few possible exceptions that I will include at the end of each section.

YOU DON'T HAVE TO FEAR
THE HOME STUDY

With few rare exceptions, prior to adopting, adoptive parents-to-be must complete an adoption home study. Since the term itself can be intimidating, some agencies have moved away from the term's use and replaced it with names that depict a warmer, friendlier process. You'll hear "adoption assessment," "adoption preparation and education," or "family assessment," but for our purposes, I will continue to refer to this process by the words most commonly recognized as the greatest source of anxiety for any pre-adoptive parent anywhere: the dreaded home study.

The home study results in an actual document, usually a minimum of ten pages long, which is used as a tool throughout an adoption. At the very least, your home study will be submitted to court when you file your adoption petition, but it could also be shared with other agencies, attorneys, courts, and, in a few states, even birthparents. Your home study is the culmination of all the information and documentation you provide to an agency or social worker compiled into one comprehensive document. Although not identical, all domestic adoption home studies contain the same basic information needed to adopt within any jurisdiction of the United States.

If I were a social worker in some other state and had never met you, I could simply read your home study (assuming it is a well-done, thorough study) and learn a sufficient amount about who you are, what you expect from the process, and if you meet all the qualifications needed to complete an adoption in my state. Without this document, it would be extremely difficult, if not impossible, to make an accurate assessment of a family so quickly.

I can understand why people are not thrilled by the idea of a social worker compiling a large document, detailing anything and everything you could ever imagine about yourself, your history, your extended family, and, yes, your extended family's history. As intrusive as this process can be, I'm sure you can understand the necessity of having a thorough evaluation of a family before bringing an infant into that home. (Or at least why any agency would want this before signing on the dotted line vouching for your wonderfulness!)

For the birthmother, a home study is reassuring proof that you are not the only one who thinks the people you've asked to become the parents of your child are wonderful; the document shows they really are law-abiding, normal citizens. From the viewpoint of the larger society, the document is essential as a safeguard tool to ensure the well-being of all children. In fact, the home study process may be the only element of the domestic adoption process that is actually quite similar in all fifty states. For the professionals handling adoptions, a thorough home study makes the process much easier and much more efficient for all.

The most common source for obtaining a home study is through a private licensed adoption agency. Depending on your beliefs, you may want to select an agency that is in line with your personal philosophy. For example, a religiously affiliated agency may conduct their home studies by asking questions that fall in line with their particular system of beliefs, which may or may not be a big deal to you. It is really just personal preference.

If you are a gay or lesbian family, an agency may prefer to write your home study in one of several ways. They may present you as a single person adopting alone and identify your partner as a "roommate" or as an "unrelated adult in the household" without ever clearly labeling this person as your partner; they may present you as a single person adopting alone legally but then reflect your relationship with your partner in the rest of the home study, or they may write your home study as a couple, identifying both you and your partner as adopting together. An agency's reasoning for choosing one of these formats over another may be influenced by one of several factors. They could be writing your study to adhere to the statutory requirements of your state (for example, if you will be completing a second parent adoption, your home study may be written with the second "updated" version needed for the second adoption in mind); they may be tailoring your study to adhere to the legal climate of the court system where you will be filing your adoption (for example, the more ambiguous cultural climate of your court); or it may be the agency's policy or customary practice to prepare their home studies in a certain way. Regardless of the rationale, it is important to ask your agency why they are writing your home study in that particular format and what particular benefit that will provide you. If you do not agree with an agency policy and cannot negotiate a compromise, you may need to find another resource that is a better fit for you.

To understand what is involved in a home study, you should think of it as a process with multiple layers. I say "layers" rather than "parts" because it is not unusual for a home study to have several different tasks or purposes all happening simultaneously. If you envision layers, you can easily imagine these tasks overlapping, while at other times they occur only one at a time or in a linear fashion. Every agency has its own preference regarding the sequence and/or duration of the layers involved, but the overall appearance and end result of a home study looks the same.

Layer 1: Information and Documentation

The first layer of a home study contains all the specific information and documentation unique to you. You will be asked to submit several documents, such as birth certificates, marriage certificates, divorce decrees, proof of income, proof of physical health, and proof that you have no serious criminal history or a history involving a child protection agency (usually accomplished through fingerprinting or some other type of background check), as well as letters of personal reference. Most often, the state's adoption code specifies the documents required by law. In addition, you may be required by law to provide additional documentation under certain circumstances. You'll need a statement from your physician confirming your ability to parent a child if you have certain health problems. If you have any prior criminal convictions, you will need to provide a written explanation of the circumstances along with any relevant legal documents; or if you have a psychological disorder, you'll need a letter from your doctor or therapist confirming your ability to parent.

In some states, every family who adopts an infant must first obtain a foster care license. This doesn't mean that these families will ever actually provide foster care for a child, but it does prove that if they are qualified to be a licensed foster parent, they are also qualified to be an adoptive parent.

In some states the requirements for adoption are vague and allow the agencies to decide what documents they want to provide to meet the statutory requirements. For many agencies, the documents they require you to submit go above and beyond what is actually required by law. The scope and number of these documents can vary widely from agency to agency. Sometimes, it is simply the preference of an agency's individual director or just "the way it's always been done" by agencies in your area. Legally, an agency must request documentation for only what is specifically required by a state's statute, but agencies will frequently ask for further documentation as a safety net.

Some common examples of additional documents an agency may require include: proof of health and/or life insurance, a written plan detailing who will care for your adopted child in the event of your premature death (commonly called a guardianship plan—this is more likely to be of greater importance if you are single or unmarried), a letter from your employer confirming your salary, job longevity and/or stability, your most recent tax return (first two pages only), proof of any debt and/or assets, a well-water test, a detailed fire escape plan, your driving record, and an agreement to refrain from using corporal punishment. If you are gay or lesbian, the agency may also ask you to provide the name of a particular person you have asked to be a male or female role model to your child.

Yes, I'm afraid that there are agencies that will require a great deal more documentation than even this. I call this "document overkill," and even though it may seem harmless enough, you may want to consider looking elsewhere for home study services if the requests seem extreme.

Layer 2: Education

The second layer of a home study is the educational component. Adoptive parents are often required to complete a specific number of training hours as a part of the home study. Some states specify the exact number of hours, while some simply refer to the completion of an "agency-approved training program" or an educational curriculum. Regardless of the number of training hours specified by a state's statutes, an agency can require additional hours if it chooses. A typical number of training hours can range from six to upward of twenty hours. Some agencies conduct periodic in-house seminars, some require their clients to read particular books and complete some kind of report, some have access to online programming, and some supply their own online training materials. Some agencies will let you choose from several topics so you can pick the ones that seem interesting or of most concern to you. Some common topics for training might include attachment and bonding with your baby; learning about open adoption; how to talk to your child about adoption; prenatal drug and/or alcohol exposure risks; race, culture, and ethnicity in adoption; and understanding birthparent grief.

As difficult as completing these hours may be, I highly recommend that you invest as much time and effort into the training materials as you can. Take full advantage of the opportunity and learn as much as you can. The more you know, the more empowered you will feel, and the less anxiety you will experience throughout the process.

I know it is difficult to focus on a distant topic, like the intuitive phase of a four-year-old, which won't impact your life for years, but try to think of adoption not as an event, but rather as a lifetime process that begins now. Families have told me that after enduring the difficulties of infertility, wandering through the overwhelming maze of adoption, and finally arriving at a place where they could see light at the end of the tunnel, they have a hard time caring about the training aspect. Instead, they want to scream at their social worker, "If you will just get this baby into my house before I retire, then I promise I will care!"

These feelings are normal, and they don't mean that you don't care; you've been through a lot and are getting a little depleted. Any social worker should understand this and try to help you plan a way to study the information when you're able to absorb it. During a home study adoptive parents are considered a captive audience and have no choice but to listen to what the social worker has to teach you. I admit, sometimes as the teacher, I knew I probably wasn't fully getting through, but because I may not get another opportunity, I had to give it my best shot. If you find yourself getting frustrated during your home study, don't just "get it over with," but ask your social worker for a list of resources that could be helpful to you later.

Layer 3: The Interview

The third layer of a home study is the interview process. Most often a social worker will meet with the adoptive couple both together and individually, as well as with any children who are already living in the home. The number and length of the meetings can vary. Some agencies complete a study in one very long marathon session, while others will meet with the family four, five, or even six times. At least one meeting will take place in your home.

Prior to the interview, agencies will ask you to complete an extensive autobiographical questionnaire, asking you for everything from providing a physical description of yourself, to describing your childhood, to expounding upon what you hope to provide for your child as a parent. These answers form the general framework of your home study document and, hopefully, by the conclusion of the interview process, your social worker will have learned all she needs to know to create a clear and accurate description of you, your household, your strengths, and your parenting abilities.

Although sometimes it might be hard to gauge completely, it can be extremely beneficial to learn something about the overall culture of the agency you are considering for your home study. Each agency has a slightly (sometimes extremely) different view on the function and purpose of a home study, and knowing what to expect can help. Here are a few questions to ask that will help you understand an agency's home study philosophy.

What is the average length of time it takes one of your families to complete a home study?

How many meetings are typically held?

How many hours of training do you require? What types of training do you offer?

Can you provide me with a list of the documents you require for a home study?

What is the administrative process for a home study to be completed/finalized/approved?

If an agency says they have a home study approval process or that a family must first be approved, it may suggest the agency has rigid policies or a philosophy that plays a paternal role in the adoption process. I once worked for an agency that provided child welfare services for more than a hundred years. It seemed to me that many of their practices hadn't evolved much during those hundred years either! As staff members, we were required to present our home study cases at a weekly meeting. We had to discuss our cases and the family was then either "approved," meaning that the adoption supervisor would sign off on the home study report and they would be able to proceed with their adoption, or the caseworker was expected to return to the family and address unresolved issues. At the next meeting, the staff member could present the family's home study a second time to gain approval.

This agency was definitely what I call "old school." Some of the staff approached every possible issue in a family with great suspicion rather than simply identifying and building upon their strengths. For example, if a couple did not appear to have grieved their infertility long enough or with enough fervor, it probably meant that they hadn't really dealt with it at all and were in denial. Or perhaps a blended family demonstrated skilled methods of communication and claimed to have made a fairly peaceful transition into a new household, so they must be hiding the real issues that without a doubt I didn't pick up on. The negative environment put pressure on me and the other caseworkers to find problems even when they didn't exist!

Gratefully, not every organization is so rigid. Look for an agency that seems flexible and is willing to tailor its guidelines to fit each situation, characteristics that indicate a more pliable, modern approach to the home study. The extent to which an agency worker understands and can articulate the difference between what is law and what is their policy or requirements will help you determine if the agency is a good fit for you.

8

Being "Put Up" for Adoption: The ICPC

Created partially in response to the unregulated trafficking of children, the Interstate Compact on the Placement of Children (ICPC) was drafted in the late 1950s in order to establish a system that monitors the legal placement of children into foster care and adoption across state lines. New York was the first state to enact the compact in 1960, and today the ICPC is in effect in all fifty states, Washington, D.C., and the U.S. Virgin Island Territories. Before a placement occurs out of state, the ICPC rules assure the placement is safe and in the child's best interest. This applies to both a child who is in foster care and under the jurisdiction of a public agency, as well as to an infant whose adoption is being arranged by a private agency or attorney. If you adopt an unrelated child who is born in another state, you will be required to comply with the rules of the ICPC.

Because adoptions frequently occur over state lines and every state and territory has its own unique set of adoption laws, ICPC's primary function is to ensure three things: the home where the child is being placed is adequate, everyone involved followed each state's laws, and responsibility can be established in the case of a failed adoption.

If you are considering an adoption across state lines, make sure you find an agency that has experience completing interstate adoptions. Interstate adoption involves a unique set of rules and requirements. Not all interstate adoptions work the same way, but here is a hypothetical example so you can gain an understanding of ICPC procedures and how interstate adoption works.

You have just completed a home study in the state where you live, Wisconsin, with the highly respected, licensed private agency White Glove Adoption Services. By using the Internet, it doesn't take long for you to connect with Katie, an expectant mother who lives in Illinois and is making an adoption plan for her baby.

Katie is due in three months and is planning to give birth in her hometown. She has not contacted any agency or attorney yet, but she tells you that she has done a great deal of research on the Internet. You send her your paper profile (or video), and the very next day she calls you back and asks to meet you. A week later, you find yourselves driving to Illinois to meet Katie and her mother for dinner. Since the dinner is a complete lovefest, she soon officially asks if you will be the adoptive parents for her baby.

Now, you know that you will need to find an agency in the state of Illinois that is not only licensed but also experienced in handling interstate adoptions. The Beautiful Bundle Adoption Agency of Illinois explains to you over the telephone that they can provide all the necessary services for both you and the expectant parents, and that you can contract with them directly (in other words, you can sign a service agreement with them and return it with a check). Beautiful Bundle will request your home study from White Glove, complete and compile the ICPC packet of documents, and submit them quickly. They will also provide Katie with her own advocate (a social worker) who will counsel her throughout the entire process. You give White Glove Katie's information and then let her know to expect a call from the advocate, Addy, within a couple of days.

Now, you contact your social worker (Polly) at White Glove and let her know about your possible adoption in Illinois. You tell Polly to expect a call from Beautiful Bundle Adoption Agency and ask that she provide them with an original home study report as well as any other documents they ask for. Polly then refreshes your memory about how the finalization process works in Wisconsin. (You did learn about this during your home study, but the truth is, you were really nervous about the fact that you didn't have time to organize your linen closet, so you weren't able to absorb everything.) Still, before you can decide which state is the best one to file your adoption in, you will need more information about Illinois.

Beautiful Bundle e-mails you a list of Illinois attorneys, which includes the disclaimer "This list does not constitute an endorsement of any party." When you ask for a recommendation, Beautiful Bundle tells you that they most often work with attorney A. Schmarty, who is highly experienced in interstate adoptions and is a member of the American Academy of Adoption Attorneys (aka a "Quad A" attorney).

Next, you call Ms. Schmarty and are relieved to find that she really does seem knowledgeable and likable. (She even insists that you call her by her first name, Anita.) She uses simple terminology to explain the legal process, and after you call three other adoption attorneys from the list, you find out that her fee is even slightly lower than the others. Ms. Schmarty offers to meet with you in person, but since you weren't planning to make the six-hour drive to Illinois again for several weeks, you decide to just go ahead and retain Ms. Schmarty and give her a retainer (like a down payment). You soon receive a detailed contract (which you actually read before signing) indicating that if the adoption moves forward following the baby's birth, you will then be required to pay the remaining balance.

After your conversation with Ms. Schmarty, you now know that it is most beneficial for you to file your adoption in the state of Illinois (also known as the sending state in an ICPC), which means the adoption will be finalized in Illinois as well. (If you lived in a state other than Wisconsin, or if you were adopting a baby born in a state other than Illinois, this might not be the case. So it is critical to discuss procedures with knowledgeable resources in both states so you are well informed.)

Meanwhile, Addy, Katie's advocate, helps her fill out all the necessary paperwork (not only for the Illinois adoption, but also for the additional items necessary for the ICPC process as well). Addy contacts the birthfather (we'll call him Pete), who says he is willing to meet and sign whatever papers are needed. He explains that because he already pays regular child support for one child, he cannot afford to support another. He thinks Katie's plan of adoption is a good idea and is happy to provide medical and social history for the child. Because it is allowed by law, Pete also signs a legal document called an "unborn surrender," which will be filed in court and will terminate his parental rights after the baby is born and after Katie has signed the same legal document.

Katie tells her adoption advocate she does not need any financial help at this time, but that she is concerned about making ends meet during the six weeks following the birth when she isn't working. Addy explains to Katie that this expense is allowable under Illinois law, so the adoptive family can place money into an escrow account at Beautiful Bundle, which Katie can use to pay her bills and expenses during those six weeks.

You believe the expense is reasonable and arrange to have the escrow account held at the Illinois agency. As part of the arrangement, the money will go directly to the party owed, for example, Katie's rent, utilities, and car insurance. This will provide evidence to the court that the expenses you pay are legally allowable.

When Katie goes into labor, you get the call and head to the hospital as soon as you can. Katie gives birth to a beautiful, healthy baby boy. After two days the hospital clears Katie to go home. Still committed to her plan of adoption, she signs a temporary custody agreement, which allows you to bring the baby directly home from the hospital. (Okay, not really home, but to the small suite at the nearby hotel where you will be staying.)

Katie's advocate is there to help with the discharge, because technically, Katie gives temporary custody of her son to Beautiful Bundle, the Illinois agency, which allows the hospital to discharge the baby to them, and in turn, the agency grants you temporary custody.

By Illinois law Katie may sign the final papers, called surrenders, anytime after the baby is seventy-two hours old. In other words, she may not sign until her baby is at least three days old. She can take as much time as she needs before signing, but once she does sign, it is final and irrevocable. The law also allows Katie to sign the papers with a representative of a licensed agency in lieu of appearing in court. Addy makes an appointment to come to Katie's house about six hours after the seventy-two-hour minimum waiting period (arranging the signing a few hours beyond the minimum time period demonstrates that Beautiful Bundle is in no way pressuring Katie to sign).

Katie is anxious to put the difficult process of signing behind her, so she completes the final surrenders with Addy just as planned. Addy then travels to your hotel to (1) give you the good news and (2) have you sign more papers that ICPC requires for their approval on your placement. Addy tells you that she will work on finalizing the paperwork right away and let you know as soon as it is ready to be sent out.

You enjoy your first weekend as parents, and even though you wish you could be home, you are making the best of it. The hotel staff is extremely kind and is helping in any way they can. (For example, whenever possible, they are leaving the rooms near yours vacant so you will not have to feel anxious about disturbing the other guests when the baby cries in the middle of the night—and the wee hours of the morning—and last night, most of the time between the two!)

On Monday morning you promptly get a call from Ms. Schmarty

who, after congratulating you, tells you that you are on the docket to appear in court on Wednesday morning at ten o'clock. She will meet you there and together you will appear in front of the judge to file the adoption officially. In Illinois, this is the one and only time you will need to appear in court. When the six-month post-placement period is over, Ms. Schmarty will submit the finalization documents on your behalf and initiate the birth certificate process with the Department of Public Health.

On Wednesday morning when you arrive at court, you meet several other families who are adopting as well, and the atmosphere is upbeat. (In fact, Anita tells you that the nickname for these hearings is "happy court.") The judge is gracious and poses for photos with you. You receive copies of the legal documents, and within an hour, the court portion of the adoption is complete. Adoption court in this county is streamlined and well organized. In smaller counties where few adoptions take place, you may have to wait much longer than an hour for a hearing.

You still cannot leave the state with the baby until the documents are approved by ICPC, so your attorney promptly sends the court documents via overnight mail to ICPC and Beautiful Bundle does the same with their packets.

The rest of the ICPC adventure usually goes something like this: The packet arrives at the ICPC the next day. It sits on the administrator's desk all day and through the weekend until it finally gets opened on Monday. The ICPC administrator requires verification from Beautiful Bundle indicating which agency will handle post-placement visits and reports.

Beautiful Bundle calls you to confirm that White Glove is, indeed, the agency conducting your post-placement reports and that three are required. Beautiful Bundle then calls White Glove and asks for a faxed document detailing this commitment. White Glove tells Beautiful Bundle they need payment from you for the third post-placement visit (since your home study fee only included payment for two) before they can fax the document. Next, Beautiful Bundle calls you again to explain the delay, you call White Glove and authorize payment of the fee electronically, then you call Beautiful Bundle to let them know the fee has been satisfied. White Glove finally faxes the commitment document to Beautiful Bundle, who in turn faxes it to ICPC in Springfield. Unfortunately for you, by the time this is all finally resolved, it is too late for the administrator to review the document. Wednesday arrives and the ICPC administrator calls to let Beautiful Bundle know that the packet has been approved by him and was sent out in the overnight envelope (postage-paid, smartly included by the administrative whiz at Beautiful Bundle) to the next ICPC office in Madison, Wisconsin, also known as the receiving state. Whew! Let's stop a moment and take a breath!

Okay, we're in the homestretch. Now that you know the packet has left Illinois, you decide to go to a hotel closer to the Wisconsin border so you can stay in Illinois with the baby, and your husband can drive home to Wisconsin, get the mail, some clean clothes, and maybe even go to into the office and catch up a little. It is okay for either you or your spouse to cross state lines, but the baby cannot leave Illinois yet.

The weekend passes. You wait through Monday with no word. You know the packet is somewhere in Wisconsin, but whether anyone has picked it up yet is anyone's guess. You call Beautiful Bundle on Monday and ask if they've heard anything. You ask (plead, really) with Beautiful Bundle to call ICPC in Wisconsin to check on the packet. They explain that they cannot call Wisconsin ICPC, only Illinois ICPC.

On Tuesday morning, one hour and forty-five minutes after your spouse left for work in Wisconsin (exactly thirty-three minutes after he arrived there), you get the call from Beautiful Bundle that you can go home.

ICPC PRACTICAL CONSIDERATIONS

Although out-of-state adoption can be complicated, recent ICPC changes in some states have made the process less cumbersome than I just described. For example, there is at least one state (and possibly more by the time you are reading this) where an ICPC packet can be submitted prior to a baby's birth. In Nevada, a child cannot be discharged from the hospital until ICPC approval is received. In Kentucky, a child must go to a "neutral home" while ICPC is pending approval. In Oklahoma, ICPC is privatized and charges a fee; however, you can get a twenty-four-hour turnaround on an approval packet. Since the ICPC process varies widely state by state, you must find an experienced professional in the sending state, or, in most cases, the state where your baby will be born.

Regardless, revised ICPC regulations are slowly making their way through each state's approval process, which will hopefully alleviate many of the inconveniences typically found in our nearly fifty-year-old compact. The new compact, called "Interstate Compact on the Placement of Children," makes provisions that will allow adoptive families to travel home prior to receiving final approval for their interstate packet and sets up new comprehensive rules for enforcement. The bad news is that the new ICPC must be enacted in thirty-five states before it can take effect, and it looks like it will take a while.

Despite the red tape associated with ICPC, it is legally necessary because it ensures that both birth and adoptive parents are not exploited. If an adoption professional assures you that ICPC is not necessary in your interstate adoption, I urge you to get a second opinion before you proceed.

9

Finding Professionals Who Truly Are

Adopting an infant can be expensive considering $20,000 is the average cost of a domestic adoption. With my advice, you will likely spend less and know exactly what each dollar you spend will accomplish. The federal tax credit, available to most families, can really help your bottom line, and many employers offer some adoption assistance benefits. Even with these added benefits, be prepared to spend some money.

CAVEAT EMPTOR

When it comes to money, my best advice is this: don't ever let your emotions get their hands on your checkbook! Wanting to be a mother (or father) is a deep and wrenching desire. Sure, your head knows that not everyone has your best interests in mind, but when your heart hears the words it has been aching to hear for years, even the most intelligent people on the planet are apt to be swayed. For someone so small, a baby wields enormous power, and that is exactly what some people in the adoption industry are counting on.

I have heard couples defend their rationale for paying huge, up-front fees to facilitators or consultants (who, by the way, they often only talked to once after finding them on the Internet!), when the only real reason they wrote the check was because they were told exactly what they wanted to hear. Some families were told that paying $25,000 in advance was simply standard procedure for "exclusive matching services."

Occasionally attorneys, facilitators, consultants, and even agencies flatly refuse to produce a written breakdown of their fees, which can exceed $20,000, with the statement, "It just isn't our policy." There are individuals and organizations who promise their clients an adoption within a certain time frame, sometimes even offering a money-back guarantee. You will never find this in writing, but one agency known for charging extremely high fees will discreetly deliver a couple's newborn baby to their home and then, in the driveway, expect payment. After many years of investigation, I am happy to report that this agency finally lost its license (at least in one state, that is).

Maybe these practices aren't truly illegal, but I have no problem calling them unethical. Where I sit as a birthmother and a professional, there is absolutely nothing worse than the people in the world of adoptions whose first and foremost goal is to make a profit. As one reputable adoption attorney recently phrased it, "They are the used car salesmen of adoption." As long as it remains difficult to regulate fifty different adoption statutes, and until the child's welfare comes first and foremost for everyone, these practices will continue.

Most adoptive parents don't like to admit that their judgment was clouded by emotion when they fall prey to these "used car salesmen." Just remember, as strange as it might sound, you are now a consumer—not a baby consumer, but a consumer of the services that will lead you to that goal.

THE OTHER VULNERABLE HALF

Agencies and other adoption representatives take advantage of birthmothers as well. Since they're so often already feeling a great deal of shame, they may (unconsciously, of course) tell themselves the mistreatment must be what they really deserve. They rarely have the resources or even the emotional energy required to defend themselves from poor business practices. I want to point out that adoptive parents rarely are culpable in situations of birthparent manipulation. Most often, it is the people in trusted positions of authority take advantage.

For example, my friend Stephanie gave birth to her daughter in the state of South Carolina in 1993. She was twenty years old at the time and a full-time college student. She had worked with an attorney to make an adoption plan for her baby, which included choosing a family that he also represented. Less than twenty-four hours after her daughter's birth, her adoption attorney approached her to sign the papers that would permanently terminate her parental rights. This practice was legal in that state, and Stephanie did sign the documents. A short time later, she regretted her decision and felt that she did not have a clear head when she was asked to sign due to being under the influence of narcotic pain medications. She says her memories of the actual event were fuzzy and even somewhat incomplete.

Stephanie did follow through with her objection legally and was granted a review in front of a judge. The judge dismissed her claim and the adoption was allowed to continue. The judge ruled that the attorney was well within the confines of the law and that the effect of the drugs alone was not sufficient as a primary cause of her change of heart.

Part of the role of an adoption agency worker in some states involves completing the surrender documents for birthmothers. Rather than having to appear in front of a judge, the law allows the papers to be completed with a qualified representative of a licensed adoption agency. The relatively simple act of signing some papers is anything but simple, considering the impact it has on the birth-mother's life forever. The agency I represented took this process very seriously and was extremely cautious in taking the necessary safe-guards to protect both the adoptive and birth family from liability. We made an audio recording of every signing, during which we asked the soon-to-be birthmother to answer a series of questions aloud, such as, "Is anyone threatening you, pressuring you, or promising you anything in return for signing this surrender?" and "Do you understand that after signing this document you cannot change your mind, reclaim, restore, or return your rights as legal parent over your child, in any way, for the rest of your life?"

Even with these careful measures in place, I still took time to walk away to give the mother space. In some cases, the new mother insisted that she wanted to continue, but I knew she wasn't ready and needed more time. It would have been perfectly legal for me to just get the job done, but would it have been the right thing to do? Was the anxious couple thrilled about this? Of course not. Did they under-stand? Yes, they did. Most couples were grateful to feel confident that the mother freely and voluntarily relinquished their child. They knew they could love their new child with total abandon and not feel guilty. Some adoptive parents feel tremendous anguish knowing that their child's birthmother really wanted to parent her child, but in some way was pressured into agreeing to go through with the adoption.

When you purchase a new home, do you think it might be fool-ish to rely only on the realtor who is also representing the sellers? Would you trust the safety of a new product if the testing scientist was married to the manufacturing company's president? It is easy to see the potential conflict of interest here, yet regularly in adoption the expectant mothers are advised by the same attorney, facilitator, or social worker who is also advising the adopting couple. It may be perfectly legal, but I do not believe it is in the best interest of the birthmother.

ASKING THE RIGHT QUESTIONS

When you consider the amount of money you will likely spend on this process and the impact it will have on your future, finding the right professionals is one of the most important things you will do. Since we established that you are, indeed, a consumer, what exactly are you paying for anyway?

The worksheets on pages 90–95 contain lists of specific questions you can ask any professional before hiring them to help you with your adoption. I recommend you use one sheet for each organization you contact. There are three lists included here: the first will help you identify an agency to complete your home study, the second will help with an actual placement (including information on interstate placements as well), and the third will help with identifying an attorney.

Read the list ahead of time and circle the numbers of each question you want to ask before you make an initial contact. Whenever possible, I have phrased the questions in a "yes" or "no" answer format. If you make a note about a specific question, check the box under "note," which will remind you to read what you've written about that particular item. Do your homework before you call by reading an organization's website or written materials. Be aware that good agencies keep relevant statistics and will know the answers to the questions I've provided; if they don't know or don't seem to want to share, it may be a red flag.

Obviously, I created this worksheet to reflect the things I consider most important. If you agree with the ideas I've presented in this book, then you will probably agree that having more "yes" answers on your sheet, the better. You do not need to ask every single person every single question listed here, so feel free to use your own best judgment.

Word of mouth is a great way to get a lead on a good home study agency. Ask anyone you know who has adopted domestically or internationally. If you don't know anyone who has adopted domestically, you can call a local office of RESOLVE, a national infertility support network that offers individual chapters in each state. They often maintain lists of adoption organizations, as well as people you can call to talk to about their experience with a particular agency.

Agencies should also be willing to provide you with a list of past client references to call. I do think you should call them, but keep in mind that any smart agency is only going to let you talk to their most satisfied customers. Still, if you ask them very specific, descriptive questions, their answers might still be useful, although you might have to read between the lines a little. Ask them questions that will give you a feeling for the culture of the agency. For example, what did they like about their social worker? What did they dislike? Probe for information with a comment like, "I've heard that the home study process is just horrible . . ." and see what they say. If they agree, find out what part they thought was the worst. If they say it was the extreme amount of paperwork they were required to complete, but you happen to be a detail-oriented-paper-work-kind-of-person, that agency might work for you. If they say that they felt very uncomfortable because their social worker asked them intrusive and personal questions (and did not explain how they related to adoption), you'll get a sense of how the agency approaches their home studies.

Ask the adoptive parents about the training they were required to complete. What was involved, how many hours did it take, and did they find it interesting? Did they have the option of completing training online or were they required to attend a formal seminar? Were they given choices of topics that seemed pertinent to them? Or did they feel like the training was just another hoop to jump through with little added value to their overall understanding of adoption? Sorry to say, if they remember much about what their training consisted of and what they learned, then it was probably better than average!

ADOPTION PROFESSIONAL I.D. SHEET
✓ Placement Agency-Interstate Adoption

Organization Name: **Date:**
City/State: **Phone/E-Mail:**
Contact Person: **Next Steps:**

ASK	YES	NO	NOTE
1. Is your agency licensed by your state?			
2. Does your agency operate under 501C-3?			
3. Is adoption the only service your agency provides?			
4. Is infant domestic the only adoption program you offer?			
5. How many domestic infant placements did you complete in the last 12 months?			
6. Of those, how many were interstate adoption placements?			
7. Of these interstate placements, in how many were you the sending state agency?*			
8. Is the director(s) a licensed social worker (preferably masters level)?			
9. Are all staff formally educated social workers? (bachelors and/or masters level)			

ASK	YES	NO	NOTE
10. Does anyone have personal experience with adoption?			
11. Did you or your organization ever function as an unlicensed facilitator or consultant?			
12. Does your agency support the belief that open adoption is best for a child?			
13. Do you have any written philosophy or agency policy regarding open adoption?			
14. Do you provide a separate advocate for expectant parents?			
15. Can your agency provide birthmother counseling only (no placement services)?			.
16. Does the placement process in your state require that I hire an attorney?			
17. Does your agency work with an attorney? If not, can you refer one?			
18. Does your agency offer any support to birthparents post-placement? What types?			
19. Will you provide a written breakdown of all fees and costs?			

ADOPTION PROFESSIONAL I.D. SHEET
✓ Homestudy

Organization Name: Date:

City/State: Phone/E-Mail:

Contact Person: Next Steps:

ASK	YES	NO	NOTE
1. Is your agency licensed by your state to conduct homestudies?			
2. Does your agency operate under a 501C-3?			
3. Is adoption the only child welfare service offered by your agency?			
4. Is infant domestic the only type of adoption your agency does?			
5. (If no) Is infant domestic adoption your largest program?			
6. Can I contract with you for homestudy and post-placement services only?*			
7. Do you offer placement facilitation for identified adoptions as well?			
8. Considering state law, may anyone adopt with your program?			
9. How many infant placements did you complete in the last 12 months?			
10. Is the director(s) a licensed social worker (preferably master level)?			
11. Are all staff formally educated social workers? (bachelors &/or masters level)			

*Some agencies do not offer individual services. They may require participation in a program inclusive of a homestudy, matching, placement services and post placement. Usually these programs charge on large fee (usually payable in several installments).

ASK	YES	NO	NOTE
12. Do any of your staff have personal experience with adoption?			
13. Do you require a written application? What is the application fee?			
14. How many meetings are required in a typical homestudy process?			
15. How many weeks does an average homestudy process take to complete?			
16. Can my study begin quickly after I send in my application?			
17. What is your homestudy fee? Any additional fees?			
18. Do you require training beyond the # of hours required by your state? How many?			
19. Do you provide training materials (sessions, materials, books etc) for homestudy?			
20. Will you (in advance) provide a list of required homestudy documents?			
21. Does the homestudy fee include post-placement visits? How many?			
22. Does a post-placement visit also include written report?			
23. Does your agency support the belief that open adoption is best for a child?			
24. Do you have any written philosophy/policy regarding open adoption?			
25. Does your agency offer any ongoing training for adoptive families post-adoption?			
26. Will you provide a written breakdown all fees and costs?			

ADOPTION PROFESSIONAL I.D. SHEET
✓ Attorney

Organization Name: Date:
City/State: Phone/E-Mail:
Contact Person: Next Steps:

ASK	YES	NO	NOTE
1. Can you provide placement services in your state?			
2. Are you a member of the American Academy of Adoption Attorneys?			
3. How many domestic infant placements did you complete in the last 12 months?			
4. Of those, how many were interstate adoption placements?			
5. How long have you been handling domestic adoptions?			
6. Do you have any experience in handling contested adoption cases?			
7. Do you have personal experience with adoption?			
8. Do you offer a separate advocate/counseling for expectant parents?			

ASK	YES	NO	NOTE
9. What is your average cost of a completed adoption?			
10. Do you charge by the hour or a flat fee?			
11. Will you provide a written breakdown of all fees and costs?			
12. Do you require a retainer? How much?			
13. Can you provide handling of any birthparent expenses?			
14. How long is the time period prior to finalization?			
15. Do I need to appear in court?			
16. What is the average time to receive ICPC approval in your state?			

Another key to identifying a quality agency is to ask families what kinds of support they have available to them now, after the adoption is long done. This post-placement support may include such things as a monthly support group, newsletter, mediation/consultation for openness issues, ongoing training opportunities, social outings such as playgroups, an annual picnic or other regular family events, or even just a social worker available to answer your questions and talk through your concerns with you. If the family knows the services exist, it shows that they at least were made aware. If they've utilized them and have had a positive experience, even better. If they have not or would not again, ask if they would share their reasons with you. How well an agency supports its clients in the long term is a telling sign of an exceptional agency.

TIPS FOR FINDING A QUALITY AGENCY

- Make sure that anything you are told verbally you request and get in writing. For example, if you are told that certain fees will not apply to your particular situation, that additional services are included with a fee, or that you will be refunded certain fees in the case of a fall-through, yet this is not clearly stated on the fee agreement, if you don't see it in writing, ask for it in writing. If you don't get it in writing, don't assume that it is true.
- Never ever pay large fees up front. A legitimate organization will never ask you to pay more than an initial application fee of a few hundred dollars. Fees in adoption may vary slightly but should all fall in generally the same range. When an organization quotes costs significantly higher than average, find out why.
- Be wary of anyone who promises you a specific amount of time in which you can expect to adopt. It's okay for an agency to provide a general time frame based on their statistics, but don't look at it as a guarantee.

- Good agencies should have a formal grievance policy established and provided to you in writing.
- Large fees should be broken down into specific services so you can see exactly what you are paying for.
- A good agency will let you pay all medical bills directly to the doctor or hospital. When you pay through an agency or attorney, you may lose your ability to negotiate costs.
- Know that if your adoption includes a state other than your own, you are subject to the Interstate Compact on the Placement of Children (ICPC). Any professional who tells you otherwise is misinformed.
- Avoid any agency, attorney, or consultant that claims an expectant mother does not need to name the biological father and is instead encouraged to write "unknown" even when that is not the case.
- Never allow any adoption professional to represent both you and the expectant mother in an adoption. It is both unethical and legally unwise.
- When seeking an attorney, look for an attorney who is a member of the American Academy of Adoption Attorneys (known as Quad A).
- Last, but absolutely not least, never do anything that you are unsure about or do not understand, simply because someone tells you to do it. If the "expert" cannot explain something to you in terminology you can understand, then you need to find one who can.

Part III
Using Your MBA (Marketing for Baby's Adoption)

10

Nice to Meet You, Ken and Barbie

Having a paper profile ready to go is the first thing you need to begin marketing as prospective adoptive parents. Even if you don't plan to launch a huge campaign blitz, if you have a profile on hand, you can respond to any leads that just, by chance, might come your way.

Every time I speak at an adoption conference, people want to know, "What was it about your family's letter that you especially liked?" or "Why did you pick your adoptive family?" Just as the questions never change, neither does the answer. Even though families never seem to be satisfied with my response, the truth is, there really isn't a magic ingredient to writing a great letter except for one—just be yourself!

Almost nothing creates more anxiety and/or misunderstanding for adoptive families as the "Dear Birthmother" letter. On one side, you, the hopeful parents, agonize over which pictures to include, how much information to share, and on and on. On the other side, we birthmothers typically don't see those things as nearly as significant. In fact, I don't think I know one birthmother who says she fell in love with her child's family because they had the fanciest "Dear Birthmother" letter.

Not to completely negate its importance, but my friend Meg says that the only reason she chose to meet her son's adoptive parents was that their letter was the only one in the stack that didn't look the same! (Luckily for everyone, it was love at first meeting.) The most important thing about a profile letter is that it accurately reflects who you are and paints a broad picture of what it would be like to be a child in your family. If you are gay or lesbian, regardless of how your home study is written, your profile should reflect the true nature of your household. So in other words, even if only one of you is going to be the legal parent of the child, if your home is a two-parent household, you will want to indicate that in your profile.

Writing a profile really doesn't have to be as difficult as people usually make it. Yes, it is an important tool; but remember, it is only one tool in a whole toolbox of things you can use, so don't invest more energy or worry than you really need to. I didn't choose Ron and Sybil from profile letters, so I don't personally understand what that would be like, but I have watched the process unfold over and over again firsthand, so I have a pretty good idea of what works well and what rarely works at all.

The most important thing about any kind of marketing in adoption is that it is an authentic, accurate reflection of who you really are. What I liked about my child's family and what another woman might like can be two very different things. I honestly do believe there is someone for everyone. My ultimate goal is to make it as easy as possible for you to find the right match.

FRANK AND KAREN

Before being green was trendy, I worked with a family who not only believed in the three R's (reduce, reuse, and recycle), they lived it in just about every aspect of their lives. Frank and Karen were proud of their values, yet others viewed them as a couple of pretty odd ducks!

Frank and Karen lived in a metropolitan area in a very modest apartment, owned in a small cooperative that had a community veg-etable garden and a large bicycle shed in the courtyard. Everyone in the building looked out for each other, much like neighborhoods years ago. In some ways, it seemed that they found a little utopia in a chaotic world.

Frank and Karen didn't own a car, but instead used public trans-portation to get them where they needed to go. When they could, they rode their bicycles. They bought all their clothing and furni-ture "gently pre-owned" and tried to choose products that mini-mally affected the environment (which, mind you, many years ago was not as easy as it is now!).

My guess is that Frank and Karen did not look like the perfect adoptive parents to many adoption agencies. When I first met them, I wondered aloud why they didn't just move to the country some-where. They both looked at me like I was nuts—I clearly didn't "get" them yet. They loved the city—the arts, the museums, the diversity—and they would never want to give that up. They simply felt satisfied by living simply in the city.

Frank and Karen were both college educated and had met while volunteering for the same not-for-profit organization. Unfortunately, they were both already in their late thirties, so by the time they finally married, they knew their biological clocks had ticked beyond making a baby. They certainly weren't wealthy, but they were wise with their finances and had plenty of savings to finance an adoption.

When it was time to write a profile letter, this couple saw no rea-son to mimic the hundred or so other letters I showed them as exam-ples, but instead produced something that was true-to-self for them. Frank handwrote the letter on pastel-colored construction paper in blue ink. They included a few photos of the things they most treas-ured: their dog, their families, and their closest friends. When Frank handed me six copies, I was more than a little surprised. No one had ever handwritten their letter before, and definitely, no one had ever written about how proud they were of not owning an SUV!

I told Frank that he would need to write out many more copies if he intended to stick to this unorthodox format. He laughed at me and remarked how funny it was that I would use the word "unorthodox," because that was exactly what he wrote in the very first line of his letter: "Dear Birthmother, I'm sure this letter looks a little unorthodox compared to the other profiles you've seen . . ." He said he would be happy to handwrite more copies (which he did).

The letter was well written, sensitive, and honest. It conveyed the couple's values, passions, and interests. Their core values, like education, honesty, and integrity were all right there, clearly spelled out. It was all the other things that made me nervous—like the fact that they believed wholeheartedly in recycling, which included that they purchased all of their clothing and furniture only from local thrift stores. I also wondered what my agency would think of the letter! My wonderful and open-minded directors agreed we could use the letter, but their practical and business-minded sides also hoped the letter wouldn't be a waste of time and money for this family.

The risk paid off. Several times I watched an expectant mom pull the stack of profiles out of the envelope and visibly react when she got to theirs. I admit that I had my reservations about whether or not I had made the right choice. I wondered if I should have insisted on saving this family from themselves.

ENTER MIRANDA AND JON

Miranda and Jon were both twenty-one years old and had met when they sat next to each other in a yoga class at the local YMCA. (Jon admitted that he signed up for the yoga class only because he was extremely shy and was told it might be a good place to meet a girl—which was obviously good advice!)

The young couple were living together in a cheap studio apartment but were still barely scraping by. Jon was a talented artist, getting a formal art education, one class at a time, which was all he could finance at that time. He also worked nights cleaning offices, but that job was sporadic, so he was looking for another job as well. Miranda worked full-time for a not-for-profit environmental group, for which she was completely passionate. She earned only minimum wage, but I think Miranda probably would have done it for less.

When Miranda found out she was pregnant, the couple was devastated. For one thing, she was on the Pill. Miranda had been born to a teenage mom, and she had sworn that she would not end up in the same boat. They decided not to terminate but were not committed to becoming parents either. This only meant they were having a baby. They went straight to the library and began researching adoption. They decided they would want an open adoption, and so they found an agency that held the same philosophy.

I have to tell you, this truly was a remarkable young couple. They both came from chaotic, dysfunctional backgrounds and moved out on their own at young ages. They had no supportive family, and, from all outside appearances, few opportunities. They did not feel that raising the child would be fair to their baby, but they also believed they had gotten pregnant after being so careful for a reason. They believed someone out there was meant to raise this child.

Maybe I should also mention that Miranda and Jon both had dreadlocks, loved music from the '60s and early '70s, and had Jon's art, made from recycled materials (well, okay, from junk!), hanging all over their apartment. They both wrote on their social history forms that their favorite hobby was to visit museums and art galleries.

Since I'm sure you see where this is going, I'll spare you the suspense! Miranda and Jon rejected all suburban-dwelling, IKEA-shopping, soccer-mom wannabes (their words, not mine) and immediately met and fell in love with Frank and Karen. The letter I was so nervous about? Jon used it in one of his art pieces and hung it in a place of honor in their apartment.

CREATING YOUR PERFECT PAPER PROFILE

Even if you plan to do all of your searching on the Internet, I still strongly encourage you to create a paper profile for several reasons. Sending an expectant mom a paper profile, even if she has already seen it on the Internet, makes you more real, giving her something tangible to hold in her hands. It also says that you care about her personally, as shown in the effort you've made to send actual snail mail. Also, to send paper mail, you must have a physical address. If a lead is not legitimate, you will quickly know by checking to see that the address given actually exists by entering it into any Internet search engine or map program. (Often you can easily cross-check the name as well by entering either the name or the address and seeing if the other opposite comes up in any of your search engine results.)

Another important function of a paper profile is that it gives other people an easy way to help you in your adoption search. Let's say you and I are dear friends and you've written a profile. I happen to have a neighbor who is a nurse in a clinic, and she occasionally meets expectant mothers who are considering adoption. Since I love you and want to be helpful, I will want to tell my neighbor that you want to adopt and give her your letter.

When my neighbor meets an expectant mother, she can share your paper profile with her. The expectant mother now has all your contact information and can proceed (or not proceed) however she chooses. This is simple networking, and the fewer steps between you and your target audience, the more likely you are to have your plan succeed. Not only is networking effective, it is one of the most cost-effective ways to connect to a possible adoption.

GREAT PHOTOS EQUAL
GREAT FIRST IMPRESSIONS

Your profile needs to include a few well-chosen photographs. This is the part of the process where you will definitely benefit from the help of several good (and brutally honest!) friends. There are three basic rules you should follow when selecting photos for your profile: they must be recent, realistic, and of relatively good quality.

Choose a Recent Photo

Yes, maybe you looked better ten years ago, but you want a recent picture that will make you recognizable to an expecting mother who you may meet in person one day. Remember, we all come in different ages, shapes, and sizes, including birthmothers. If you have been blessed with great genes (or a great workout routine!), don't hesitate to put your best foot forward—or a well-defined arm muscle as the case may be!

Choose Shots that Reflect Your Everyday Life

"Real" for most people means casual—if casual is your usual, that is. You may have to have some new shots taken for this occasion, but rather than making an appointment with a professional photographer, ask your friend or neighbor to take a dozen or so shots in your backyard. You don't want to use overly staged photos, glamour shots, or professional photos that look artificial. Something like a wedding photo is certainly appropriate, but probably not as your first or main photo.

Realistic also means that your photos should primarily depict the typical and seemingly ordinary features of your life, with a dash of excitement thrown in. It is a documented fact (documented by me, right now, after fifteen years of reading "Dear Birthparent" letters, that is!) that childless professional couples take absolutely fabulous vacations! Most of you have seen and done some pretty remarkable stuff, and that's great. I'm not saying that it isn't okay to include a photo of you standing on a volcanic rim in Hawaii or hiking in the Costa Rican rain forest, but if no one has broken this to you yet, I'm afraid I'll have to be the first: trips like those probably won't be happening with quite the same frequency after you have a child in your home. Since I'm assuming you are looking forward to a life of diapers and *Baby Einstein*, you can probably also understand why photos of your home, extended family, pets, or even the park down the block would be more relevant to an expectant mother than a ten-page pictorial of your last wine-tasting tour in Sonoma.

Use Relatively Good Quality Photos

Forgive me if I seem patronizing, but when I say photos of "good quality," I really do mean that you should avoid out-of-focus, shot from a quarter mile away, cut-off-the-top-of-your-head photos. Even if you are the worst photographer alive, the fact that you can now take thirty quick digital pictures and then delete twenty-nine if needed has increased your chances of success dramatically. Settling for poor quality photos won't give the kind of first impression you want. In the case of your profile, using two great photos is better than including ten that are bad.

There is no magic number of photos to include, although there are a few specific things you should try to cover. Your first photo serves as the initial focus and introduction. It should at least be a standard-size print (three by five or four by six), should include only the primary members of your family (pets included if that applies to you!), and, as I stated above, recent, realistic, and of good quality. Avoid full-body shots for this one and instead use a head shot or, at most, no more than torso up, as you want your smiles to be the focus of your first impression. Try to make it natural, happy, casual, and reflective of your personality—as I always say, one where you are "smiling with your eyes as much as with your mouth." This is where a good friend's opinion can come in very handy. Even if the one photo everyone overwhelmingly loves is the one photo you especially hate, use it anyway. Often we are the worst judge of our own appearance.

PHOTO DO'S

- A group picture showing your extended family
- Photo of the outside of your house
- Photo of you with children and/or babies (playing with children is even better!)
- Photos showing your hobbies and/or activities. Examples: fishing, boating, bicycling, golfing, and so on
- Photos depicting a family tradition. Examples: a birthday party, Christmas celebration, Thanksgiving dinner, a summer cottage, and so on
- One photo of your wedding day.

PHOTO DON'TS

- Professional posed photos
- Photos with alcohol/beer bottles or cans in the background
- Identifying photos. Examples: decorative items of your last name, your street sign, or subdivision sign/name
- Photos of objects as the primary focus, such as a car, a boat, or any other prized possession
- Photos involving hunting and/or any gun hobby
- Photos depicting a particular religious ceremony
- Photos of you as a child

A Logical Layout

Use a paper profile format that can be easily reproduced at a copy shop since you will be sending out multiple copies. I like a three- or four-page letter with color photos printed on a 17 by 22-inch piece of paper in the style of a newsletter. This format looks clean and professional, and eliminates the need to staple or attach the pages together. You can easily fold it and mail it in plain white business-size envelopes. (Some expectant mothers are concerned about confidentiality and a large envelope may attract unwanted attention.)

There are many computer programs that can help you create a newsletter without too much difficulty. If you aren't computer savvy, find someone who is and either ask them to teach you or ask them to create it for you. Today, many scrapbook enthusiasts assemble their albums in digital format. Don't underestimate how honored someone may feel to be asked to help with something as important as your adoption. If all else fails, pay someone. You want someone who is knowledgeable in digital design and layout. Someone who does web design or graphic arts is overkill; someone who knows how to digital scrapbook might be just what you need. Believe it or not, there are many people in the business of specifically helping people with their adoption profiles. Enter "Dear Birthmother Adoption Letter Help" into a search engine and you might be surprised. It will be well worth the investment. You can also see some examples of paper profiles at my website: www. jenniferpedley.com.

If you have read any profile letters online, you probably know that most of them are incredibly similar. Feel free to use a basic format, but don't be afraid to mix it up a little, just as long as you cover all the subjects I list below. The biggest complaint I have heard from birthparents regarding profile letters is that they are all the same. Some agencies actually require that a family follow a specific template (maybe so no one has an unfair advantage), but these letters feel like you're reading a series of fill-in-the-blank, mad-lib puzzles!

Use Well-written Copy

The written text of your profile is probably your biggest challenge. I mean, behind every good writer is a great editor! It is important that you use proper grammar, correct all typos, and avoid vernacular that is so regional or culturally specific to your area that someone living in another part of the country might not understand. Ask several trusted people to read your letter and give you feedback. Be open to constructive criticism (as long as it is indeed constructive), and remember that it is okay to ask people who know nothing about adoption for feedback. As long as they know a lot about English, you can just smile and nod when they give you crazy advice on your adoption, and then steer the conversation back to whether you should use "lay" or "lie" in that sentence! Specifically related to adoption, include the following topics:

Why are you adopting?

This is an obvious question, but one that you might not be sure how to answer. Most important, you should be honest and open without too much detail. If you met your partner too late in life to have biology on your side, say that. If you have a health-related issue that would make pregnancy unwise for you, say that. If you have absolutely no idea why the baby-making process didn't work for you, by all means, say that too!

Don't be afraid to talk a little about infertility treatments, if that has been your experience. This is one topic that expectant mothers always wonder about but are usually too afraid to ask. Infertility may be a mystery to us, but feeling that your body has betrayed you is not. This shows her that your life hasn't gone exactly the way you thought it would either.

For example: "After three years of seeing infertility doctors, we have come to the conclusion that having a biological child is not the way our family was meant to be created," or "We have been through a great deal of heartache, including several miscarriages, but finally, adoption feels like something to be hopeful about."

If you have had a previous child (or children) by birth or through adoption, talk a little about that, such as, "After being blessed with our first biological daughter, we found we were unable to become pregnant again," or "Due to complications during my first pregnancy, our doctors have told us that having another child by birth would be unwise for us."

Already being a parent does not place you at a disadvantage to adopt. Relate your experience in a positive light. If you have given birth to a child, you could say, "Having experienced being pregnant myself, I feel an enormous amount of respect for what you are choosing for your baby." If you have adopted a child previously, reference that by saying, "Adopting our son was the best thing we ever did; we feel nothing but love for his birthmother."

No matter how you became a parent, address why you want more children. Perhaps you came from a large family and loved having siblings, or you were an only child and always wished you had brothers and sisters. Siblings are a large consideration for any expectant mother choosing an adoptive family. She might prefer that her baby be the first or only child in a family or she may only want a family where her child will have siblings (either already present or at some point in the future), but it is common that she will have some kind of preference.

When I met Ron and Sybil they were already parenting a three-year-old, which greatly influenced my decision to choose them. I could easily imagine my child in their family and predict how they would treat him. I have a vivid memory of Ron playing with Marcus in their swimming pool only a day or so after we first met. My own father never had a lot of patience, so the thought of having a playful father for my child was something I loved. That said, I don't think a family with a child was on my list of prerequisites, but just seeing Ron with Marcus made me realize it instantly.

Who are you?

I'm sure this also seems like an obvious question, but I ask it because a lot of people enter into the profile process with the answer of "Who do I need to be?" or "Who will an expectant mother want me to be?" Let's face it, writing a letter about yourself is awkward and difficult, and the fear of rejection can be paralyzing. So why would you not only sign up for it but also pay money for the privilege? Remember, you are writing to expectant mothers who feel just as insecure as you. If your profile is "rejected," it is not a reflection of your personal value; it is just another step on your journey toward getting the child you are meant to have. Perspective is always a good thing to keep around!

So back to "Who are you?" You can answer this question by recounting some basic facts: where you grew up, your family of origin, education and profession, how old you are, when you were married, where you live now, and anything else you'd like to include. Next, talk about your personality and character traits. Be as specific as possible to describe what makes you unique. For example, instead of just saying, "I have a good sense of humor," say, "I have a very dry wit and can usually make light of even the most disastrous situations." Add some random, interesting trivia about yourself, factors like your favorite foods, movies, and kinds of music. Don't underestimate the value of describing the quirky things that make you, you!

How you view yourself may be different from how others view you. You can certainly talk about that too: "My friends say I'm a very good listener." It is okay to admit to some shortcomings as well; there are always things about ourselves that others can relate to, for instance, "You will never hear me sing unless I am alone in the shower or the car. My husband says I couldn't carry a tune if it were in a bucket!"

Make sure to touch on your hobbies, talents, and interests. This doesn't mean only the things you excel at, but also just what you simply enjoy. For instance, you could say, "In my spare time, I enjoy baking, going for long rides on my bicycle, and shopping for shoes with my girlfriends," or "Physical fitness is very important to me; last year I competed in three triathlons."

Don't just say that you enjoy reading, but share what genre of book you enjoy, who your favorite author is, and the name of the last great book you finished. You never know when you could be passing on an opportunity to connect through something you might think is an insignificant detail.

Write a paragraph about your spouse, and ask your spouse to do the same for you. The paragraph should include what you love about each other and why you believe your spouse will make a wonderful parent. This paragraph should confirm to the birthmother that your relationship is stable and you are ready for children.

The last part of "Who are you?" should include something about your beliefs, morals, and values. Again, this is something that is of great interest to expectant mothers. Make sure to be forthcoming in this area. If you present yourself as neutral, impartial, and having no individual views, you don't give an expectant mother anything to identify with. At the same time, present your beliefs as belonging to you while avoiding judgment on differing views.

You can discuss how you value education, a good work ethic, and the importance of honesty. Beyond that, you might want to describe the reason you hold a specific value dear, for example: "My parents sacrificed a great deal so I could be the first in our family to go to college, and because of their example, I, too, believe that a college education should be a priority."

Truthfully describe values and morals specifically related to your religious beliefs and practices, but do not use language that may alienate someone who isn't familiar with your faith or who may have a negative association with any religion. Don't simply say that you are "Christian" or "Jewish," but instead describe how that translates in your home. "We attend services each week at a Christian church. We have many friends there, and we volunteer in a program that provides tutoring to inner-city children," or "We are of the reformed Jewish faith, which means we go to our local synagogue on Jewish holidays and celebrate our rich Jewish tradition and heritage with our families."

If you do not hold any specific religious beliefs or subscribe to any particular faith, describe this as well: "Although we do not practice any organized religion, we describe ourselves as spiritual people and feel it is important to live honest lives," or "We do not practice any particular religion but plan to expose our child to many different views and allow him or her to make that decision at an older age."

Whatever your particular story, do not worry that you will be perceived as being too pious, immoral, or whatever it is you're most afraid of. There is no way to predict what an expectant mother is looking for, and even if you could predict, what she ultimately chooses may not be what she thought she wanted anyway.

When I was looking for adoptive parents for my baby, I definitely would not have put "conservative" on my list of important qualities I wanted in a family; in fact, I probably would have told you exactly the opposite. Yet the family I fell in love with was far more conservative than I am even today. It's perfectly fine with me that we hold some differing views. Regardless, I believe they provide a great home for my child.

What would it be like for my child to grow up in your family?

An expectant mother chooses adoption for her baby, at least in part, because she isn't able to provide the kind of life she wants her child to have. If your letter paints a picture of life in your family, as well as the special memories you hope to create, it will give her more information to help her make her decision.

Describe some of the traditions you have in your family. This includes the significant events, such as celebrating holidays and birthdays, but also the more ordinary practices of family life: Will you have family dinner together each night? Will you read stories together before bed? Maybe you would like to share your plans to continue a certain tradition your father began with you when you were a child.

Will you work or be a stay-at-home mom? If you don't know yet, say so in the letter. If you have narrowed down child-care options, describe your overall plan.

Outline some of the family activities you hope to do together: Do you enjoy boating? Do you ski? Do you go to the pumpkin patch or the apple orchard each autumn? Mention your talents and skills that you would like to teach your child. Are you athletic? Do you play the guitar? Are you a skilled handyman? Are you a good cook?

Everything in your letter should work together toward painting a realistic scene of a child in your home. It isn't about having the biggest house, going on the best vacations, or all the wonderful toys you will buy. In fact, I promise you that most women are not attracted to a letter that focuses on only the external "stuff" and neglects the heart and soul of what makes a family a family. If you worry about keeping up with the Joneses, just stop! If you lined everyone up in order of your particular, perceived measure, there would always be someone with more of whatever it is you think you lack. The good news is, that person with "more whatever" is no more apt to connect with an expectant mother than you or anyone else. Remember, the expectant mother for you is already out there looking for you; your job is just to make sure she finds you!

What do you think about adoption and my role as birthmother?

It is important to talk about what you have learned about adoption and how you see adoption affecting your family. Talk about your extended family and their excitement about a new baby coming into the family. If there are other members of your family who have adopted, be sure to point that out too.

Give some basic explanation of how you plan to talk about adoption in your home, such as, "We plan to be honest and open with our child about adoption from day one," or "Our child will always know that you love him (or her) very much and that you hold a special place in our hearts."

Since you cannot know what your particular relationship will look like, communicate in general terms the things you do know and what you hope for. Indicate why you believe open adoption is beneficial for a child. Explain that kids who are adopted often do want to know their birth family, and that no matter what, the birthmother will always be an important part of your family tree.

Feel free to say you hope to have some kind of an ongoing relationship with her, if that is your hope. If you have strong feelings related to contact, don't be afraid to invite her to be a part of your lives in more concrete ways. You are less likely to scare someone off by offering too much contact than if your letter gives the impression that you are frightened by it.

Through the letter, families are likely to be the first people to introduce the concept of open adoption to an expectant mother. You may even need to reassure her that open adoption is something you really do want, because her biggest fear probably includes intruding on your family.

Many families are worried about confidentiality and ask me how much detail they should include in their letter. If you truly want to remain anonymous—meaning you do not want the letter to include the name of the city where you live or a photo of your house—then this type of open adoption may not be for you.

Anonymous?

My friend Holly made an adoption plan for her son, David, almost ten years ago. At the time, Holly did not know her son's new last name or where he lived. She understood the family's fears, and, like many birthmothers, she didn't want to intrude. When David was only two months old, Holly received some pictures of him sitting with his family in front of their fireplace. After looking at the photo several times, she noticed a decoration on the fireplace mantle in the shape of old-fashioned, lettered wooden blocks. She suddenly realized that the blocks clearly spelled out her son's new last name. Of course, she was glad to have the information, but she decided not to say anything about the discovery to the family. More than a year later, the family decided to shed their anonymity and sent Holly a letter containing their last name and address. When she revealed she had already known all along, but wanted to be respectful of their privacy, it only confirmed what they had already decided for themselves—that Holly was trustworthy.

Another birthmom I know has a similar story. In her case, the agency failed to remove the family's address label before forwarding a letter on to her. This birthmom held on to her son's identifying information for twelve years before her son's family revealed their information. In all those years, she never drove past her son's house, not even just out of curiosity to see where he lived. It certainly wasn't because she didn't want to; she'd only thought about it a million times (a day!). In tears, she told me she could not give in to that temptation, believing the act would only justify the parents' fears. That was something she was determined never to let happen.

There is generally no need for adoptive parents to remain completely anonymous. If your situation has extraordinary circumstances, then by all means get a professional involved to act on your behalf to help you remain anonymous. For the rest of you (who either aren't famous or in the witness protection program), I'll advise you on how to use common sense to safeguard your information.

COMMONSENSE CONFIDENTIALITY

There is no need for you to include your last name in your initial profile letter. Chapter 11 will advise you to get a telephone number to use specifically for your adoption process. If you'd like, you can also get a post office box rather than use your personal address for correspondence. If you use a commercial mailbox store versus the post office, your return address will be the physical street address of the store rather than an impersonal post office box number.

One other thought about confidentiality: if you choose to omit some specific, detailed information from your profile, like the name of the college you attended or the town where you grew up, you could also miss an opportunity to connect with a birthmother over a shared commonality. As crazy as this might sound, many birthmothers say some seemingly insignificant detail in a letter caught their eye and prompted them to read further. Reference to a certain college or hometown can pique a birthmother's interest. You don't want to miss out on the perfect opportunity to connect with someone.

11

Surf's Up—Making Friends with the Internet

I readily admit that I do not know how I survived before the Internet. My daily life has become completely dependent on my ability to log on, communicate, and conduct commerce and get what I need (and want) now! If I had to list the top ten important things that keep my life moving, my iPhone would, no doubt, fall within the top three. I am only mildly embarrassed to admit that last week I sent a text message to my husband, who was working in our home office, telling him that my car wouldn't start . . . from the garage.

Not surprising, the Internet has dramatically changed adoption too. With a little training, it offers limitless possibilities in your adoption marketing efforts. There are probably hundreds of thousands of social networking sites—sites with the sole purpose of bringing people together. People meet their spouses through Internet sites every day, so it makes sense that expectant moms would look to a website to find the perfect family for their babies too.

SETTING UP A SAVVY SITE

I recommend you create your own personal website that includes multiple pages with all kinds of information about yourself. Today's software programs, most hosted on the Internet so you never even have to download anything onto your computer, make it surprisingly easy to construct a clean and straightforward website without requiring you know any fancy computer programming language. You can find any number of resources to host your page for free or nearly free. Unless you are planning to use your website for more than a simple marketing tool, you honestly do not need to pay any large fees to make this work. Enter "free easy personal web page" into a search engine or go to Yahoo, Google, AOL, or any other well-known Internet presence. They all offer some kind of free, personal web page hosting.

Once you identify a place to host your site, you can begin adding content. You can easily fill two pages with the same information already in your paper profile. You can add a third page for some additional photos, and on a fourth page, you can post some basic educational information about adoption; for example, you could define open adoption and talk about why you have chosen to pursue this kind of adoption. Make a list of positive adoption language or terms that have replaced the more outdated, negative ones. List some famous adopted people or adoptive parents. Think about what you would like any potential birthmother to know. Think about what you were surprised to learn when you first started researching adoption, because a birthmother looking at your site may be surprised to learn them too.

Once you have a website constructed and have a website address, you should place links to your site everywhere you can. Include it in your family holiday newsletter (or if you have never sent a holiday family newsletter, start!). When your web address is posted on another website, like a blog or a chat room, people can click on it and land at your site.

In addition, you should also write your website's address on your profile letters and include it in the signature line of every e-mail you send. Use a short and sweet signature line, for example, "Joyfully

Hoping to Adopt a Newborn, Sally and Mike," and even have it printed on business cards. Give the cards to everyone you know and put them on every community bulletin board you find. Look for websites that already exist for couples who are hoping to adopt. They usually contain a small photo, tagline, and a link to each couple's individual website, and placing a listing on these sites is often absolutely free.

Besides having your own website, create your own page on social networking sites like Facebook, MySpace, or CafeMom. Use your page for the exclusive purpose of getting the word out that you are hoping to adopt. Social networking sites are a great way to easily connect with an enormous audience!

Anyone who wants to know more about you can find all the information they need by simply clicking on your link or typing in your web address. You can provide your adoption telephone number with an invitation to call (more about this in Chapter 13), or only offer e-mail as the method of contact. I suggest you use both to cover all the bases.

ADOPTION NETWORKING SITES

If creating your own web page seems overwhelming or time-consuming, don't worry. Many people think it makes little sense to reinvent what's already been done, so if this is you, using an existing website to post your information may be a good place to begin your Internet marketing. There are many websites dedicated to adoption marketing that are open to anyone. Be aware that some websites appear to offer independent services that are actually agencies or organizations advertising on behalf of their program clients only. A handful of large agencies that have established an extensive web presence and advertise relentlessly give the impression that they are multiple entities, when, a few clicks later, you will realize that you've circled around again, landing back at the main agency website.

Look for an independent site, meaning its only purpose is to advertise a family's adoption information—not to take part in any type of adoption or placement. Some of these sites are free and some offer their services for a fee. For example, http://www.adoption.com has a very good affiliate site called "Parent Profiles" (www.parent-profiles.com). It charges a monthly fee to host your profile. This site generates a great deal of Internet traffic because of its name.

Each site lists its own set of requirements, often found in the "user agreement" section. For example, www.parentprofiles.com can only be used by married couples who have already completed their home studies. (You must provide a copy of this document as proof, prior to posting on the site.) If you are single or gay, http://www.abcadoptions.com and www.adoptiononline.com are good choices. I've included a list of some of these sites in the back of this book.

The biggest and most visible adoption marketing websites were created for the sole purpose of generating revenue. They are generally very well organized, monitored, and regulated. Their requirements vary, as well as their fees. Some offer different price packages containing various choices, ranging from posting a basic profile letter along with a certain number of pictures to adding additional pages of photo albums, a blog, journal, or fancy fonts and other embellishments. Of course, the more services you use, the higher the monthly user fee. My usual advice is to pass on purchasing a majority of these add-ons and just commit to the basic services (as long as that includes several photographs). If an expectant mother connects with you after seeing your profile online, chances are it wasn't because you spent an extra $13.95 on the upgraded font package! Certainly, you can put that $13.95 to better use elsewhere.

These sites offer the huge benefit of great exposure. The downside is you are one of three hundred or so other hopeful adoptive couples. Keep in mind, after a user narrows her search with specific search criteria such as geography, age, or religion, the number of families drops dramatically. Clearly, the positives of gaining high visibility outweigh the negative aspects of being a small fish is a very large pool.

POST YOUR MOST POSITIVE

I suggest you go online to a website like http://www.parent profiles.com and check out your "competition." While you are looking around, rather than trying to identify the things you especially like about other families' profiles, look instead for the things that you don't like. I'm not quite sure why, but I find using this kind of critical thinking always gives me much better insight into what makes a good presentation, simply by preventing me from making the same mistakes as other people did. The first thing you will probably notice on these sites is the small "thumbnail" photos posted alongside a small "teaser" line. When you open this page, pay attention to where your eyes are drawn first. Which photo did you notice first? Was it a bright color? Was it someone's smile? Then look at the photos that your eyes passed right over. What makes these photos so unremarkable? Use this information to select your photo. Make sure your intro photo catches the eye; it matters much less where your photo lands on the page in my opinion, and eliminates the need to pay extra for "exclusive placement."

A good first impression photo should be close-up with your spouse, with just your faces filling the entire square. (Be sure the quality of your photo allows for this amount of cropping without becoming blurry.) A person should not have to go to your profile in order to see what you actually look like. Your smiles should be natural, not forced. Use a picture that makes you look happy or even shows you laughing rather than simply smiling for the camera. (Think "candid.") Never use a full-body shot for these intro photos.

I saw a bad example of a photo of a couple, obviously on some exotic vacation, riding together on an elephant. The elephant looked great, but unfortunately, I could barely make out Mr. and Mrs. Speck who were sitting on its back!

Before signing up with any site, read its user agreement (that would be the page with the very tiny print—yes, read it!) and do a little research of your own to see if other users have been happy with the service provided by the site. One way you could do this is to post your inquiry on an adoption-related discussion board. Like anything, people are much more likely to complain than compliment, so you are more likely to find information about an organization that does not have a good reputation.

INITIAL INTERNET CONTACT

When using the Internet as a means of marketing, it is likely that e-mail will be the first communication you have with an expectant mother. Remember that information or emotion can be misinterpreted in writing, so try to keep initial e-mails friendly and somewhat generic.

From my experience with contacts that begin with e-mail, potentially successful matches quickly advanced to other, less impersonal forms of communication. If someone seems satisfied with simply e-mailing back and forth with you over a long period of time, that is probably what they are really only interested in—having someone to e-mail. After the initial contact, try to move on to the next step of communication, such as a telephone conversation. After a brief, positive e-mail exchange, ask the expectant mother to call you. If she doesn't acknowledge your request or she doesn't follow through with a call after a couple of attempts, stop exchanging e-mails. Some people respond to e-mail just to get attention, with no intention of following through.

CONSIDER A VIDEO PROFILE

The final aspect of Internet marketing I want to talk about is a relatively recent phenomenon of posting a video. Unless you are one of the six people left in the world who have not been wasting hours of otherwise perfectly useful time watching videos on the Internet, then you know what I am talking about. The YouTube revolution has transformed the way amateurs seek to get discovered and how scouts find new talent. Success is now measured in the number of "hits" your video gets, which, by the way, is nothing remarkable until you get more than five or six million!

Recently, a birthmother revealed that she chose her baby's parents because of the video profile she saw. It is easy to understand why video would be preferred over paper because it brings the prospective adoptive families "to life" for the expectant mother. The quality of your video need not be professional, as long as you say something that matters and it is a fair portrayal of your family.

Don't be intimidated by the thought of portraying yourself on video. With some good preparation and a little editing, a three-minute video could definitely increase your chances of finding a birthmother more quickly and effectively than a paper profile alone.

Most home computers have the capability to burn CDs. You can copy your video onto a CD and send it in the mail as you would your paper profile. You can also post your video on the Internet, protected with a password if you prefer, and then simply give expectant mothers the password to access your video from a computer. My hunch is that the next "new norm" will be websites that host adoption profile videos specifically catering to expectant mothers where you will be able to post your own, much like the sites that host written profiles today.

I recently took an informal poll of twenty birthmothers, asking them if seeing a video of their child's adoptive family would have made it easier to choose and reduce the anxiety involved with meeting them for the first time. The overwhelming response was "absolutely!" When asked if they would prefer to see paper profiles or videos (even if they were two entirely different groups of families), they all said they would choose videos.

One friend of mine, who found her family's profile on the Internet, met three families in person before choosing the one who would ultimately adopt her daughter. Had she seen a video first, she would have not only reduced her own stress level but also spared the other two families the heartbreak of not being chosen. According to her, seeing a video would have been as effective as a face-to-face meeting.

12

Putting It on Paper: Print Ads

My favorite scene in the 2007 movie *Juno* was the one when her friend suggested she look for an adoptive family for her unborn baby in the *Pennysaver* newspaper ads.

"They have ads for parents there?"

"Yeah, desperately seeking spawn!"

And my next favorite scene is when Juno's dad meets the prospective adoptive parents and compliments them on their ad: "Oh, wicked pic in the *Pennysaver*, by the way. Super classy—not like those people with the fake woods in the background. Honestly, who do they think they're fooling?"

The *Pennysaver* is the name of a free newspaper, organized nationally but distributed locally, to small towns all over the United States. The *Pennysaver* is just one of the many publications where families hoping to adopt can regularly place classified ads to attract the attention of an expectant mother. Families call one central office to place their ad in a group of papers or in a region. And believe me, these ads really work.

Don't discount the opportunity to advertise in the free local "shopper" or newspaper in your area. You can find listings for local jobs, used cars, free kittens, neighborhood garage sales, and just about anything for sale that you could possibly want or need.

Many of these papers have a column in the classified section entitled "Adoption" or "Adoption Wanted." If there isn't a specific heading for "Adoptions," look in the "Personals" or "Miscellaneous" columns. Some adoption ads looking for birthmothers are vague but will give a toll-free telephone number to call—usually right after the phrase "all expenses paid." You will also find other shorter and more cleverly worded ads, also giving a toll-free number to call, but clearly from actual couples hoping to find their own Juno. This is exactly what I am going to teach you to do too. Not everyone owns a computer, so an expectant mother—especially one who lives in a rural area—will pick up a free copy of the *Thrifty Nickel* from one of the several small businesses in her town where this paper is delivered. Everyone has read the ads before and, like Juno, knows exactly where to find what she's looking for.

Note to Gay and Lesbian Families

My advice to you on the subject of print ads is somewhat different than what I would give a traditional family. Some of the reasons that make print ads a great way for people to connect with an expectant mother may not be the best avenue for a nontraditional family (with the exception of gay and lesbian community publications). Forgive me for generalizing, but these papers are usually found in small towns where nontraditional families make up a tiny part of the average population. As you might guess, an expectant women living here would probably still consider the concept of a gay or lesbian couple adopting children (at best) somewhat unusual. Your money would be better spent using resources that will market you within more targeted populations of the United States where two moms or two dads is not completely out of the ordinary. Websites that list nontraditional families' profiles, publications distributed within the gay and lesbian community, or simple word-of-mouth networking are strategies I would recommend most.

Getting Your Ad Noticed—First Is Best

You are more likely to get noticed, or at least receive more calls, if your ad appears first in a column. Newspapers vary in how they decide to place ads. Here are some of the more common approaches.

The No-System System: Some papers don't have any set procedures they must follow. The decision may be at the discretion of the paper's lay-out person. (This person may also be the entire sales department, or in other words, the person you are already talking to.) The easiest and most obvious way to get your ad placed first is to ask, "Can mine be first?"

First-Come-First-Serve: Some papers design their ad layouts as they receive them and simply use filler for the empty space left at the end. If you always place your ad well in advance of the deadline date, you will have a better chance of appearing first. Occasionally, if you ask, the paper may be willing to adjust their current place-ment of ads, moving yours to the top. Frankly, it often just depends on the person's willingness to be helpful and/or how difficult it is to change the current layout. Remember, it never hurts to ask.

Alphabetical Order: Some papers alphabetize their ads in a column by the first word. This makes perfect sense when you are listing used cars for sale, but this is much less useful when it comes to adoption ads. In order to make this system work to your advantage, there are a couple of key issues to consider. Obviously, if a column's ads are alphabetized, you would be wise to choose a title line that begins with the letter A. If you always begin your ads with a phrase like, "A Baby to Love" or "A Baby Is Our Dream," your ad will begin with the three letters, A-B-A, which will place your ad before any others that begin with the word "Adoption" (since the first three letters of adoption are A-D-O). Some people tack the letters "AAA" onto the beginning of the ad to insure good placement, but I really think it is somewhat confusing and don't recommend it.

Column Titles

One question you must ask any paper before placing your ad is, "What is the title of the column where the adoption ads appear?"

Some papers use a heading entitled "Adoption," but some use other heading titles such as "Personals." In papers that place adoption ads under the heading "Adoption," you will not have to include the word "Adoption" in the title of your ad. A reader will understand from the column's name what you seek.

If the column heading is anything other than "Adoption," you must add this word to clarify your ad's purpose. This small detail is critical, and here's why: if your ad is under the title "A Baby to Love" in the personal column, a person reading it may get a very different impression of what you're looking for than if your ad reads, "A Baby to Love—Adoption." Without the word "adoption," you might get some interesting phone calls!

If You Can't Be First, Be the Best

If there is no way to ensure that your ad will be first in a paper's column, you should do your best to create visibility. The number of adoption ads running with your ad influences visibility. If your ad is one of only two or three, you don't need to spend extra money on embellishing it for greater visibility. If the paper already has, say, six ads running, then you will definitely want to take further steps to make your ad stand out from the others.

Papers offer a variety of graphics intended to make your ad more prominent. You may have a choice of clip art to choose from, such as a teddy bear, an angel, or a heart. You can also embellish the text with a line border, or maybe you can outline your entire ad with tiny hearts. Some papers will allow you to include a small headshot at the top of your ad. This may cost extra, but I always recommend it. Other suggestions for greater visibility include:

- Use a larger font or bold font for just part of, or for your entire, ad.
- Separate a part of your ad with a bold, dashed, or dotted line.
- Insert extra blank lines into your ad.
- Use reverse font for part or your entire ad.

CLASSIFIED AD FORMAT

When writing a classified ad, I recommend using a basic format that can be easily adapted for different papers.

From this ad, we know the newspaper does not have a specific column for adoption ads, because the word "Adoption" is used in the heading. Second, this newspaper places ads in alphabetical order because the phrase "A Baby to Love" precedes the word "Adoption."

This ad appeared in a newspaper with the heading "Adoption," although we cannot be sure if the ads are listed alphabetically. We can speculate that the newspaper does not use alphabetical order because the people who placed the ad made an effort to increase its visibility by having it printed in reverse font. In any case, the reverse font is an excellent choice to make your ad jump off the page!

THE ART AND SCIENCE OF AN ADOPTION AD

Writing a good ad is part science, part art. You want your ad to be catchy, warm, engaging, and personal. Make sure to include your ad's purpose, provide a brief summary of yourself, and give an expectant mother specific directions on how she can contact you— all in about twenty-six words.

Follow my four-step formula to write a fabulous ad. Step 1 is to create a short three- or-four-word header. If you use the guidelines outlined in the previous section, you will want to choose words that begin with the letters A-B-A, like these, "A Baby Forever," "A Baby in Our Hearts," or "A Baby Makes Three."

Step 2 is to identify yourself by adding a descriptive detail: "We're a happily married teacher and veterinarian," or "We're a professional couple who love to snowboard," or "We've been married for ten years and both come from large families." If there are aspects of your life that pertain particularly to children or parenting, include these facts. If you are a teacher, a pediatrician, have fifty nieces and nephews, or are planning to be a full-time mom (or dad), use this information in your ad to show that you have a special affinity for children. If you have an interesting occupation, include it in your ad. If your job title only communicates "boorrring!" you might be better off simply describing yourself as a "professional."

Step 3 of your ad should reach out to an expectant mother and communicate a feeling of empathy and compassion. Phrases like "We admire your courage," "Your decision shows great strength," or

"Your love for your child is clear" illustrate that you recognize the agony an expectant mother experiences when making this difficult decision, and it also shows that you are acknowledging the connection the expectant mother has with her child.

Step 4 is the wrap-up and invitation. An open adoption tends to be more successful than one that begins with a traditional agency because of the open communication. Provide a clear indication that you hope she will contact you directly. The short yet powerful statements, "Feel free to call anytime," "Call us at home," or "Call us directly," are big reasons why this process works. Ads from consultants and attorneys are often ambiguous and unclear, leaving the reader wondering who it is they would actually be calling. Your invitation should make it clear that the number you're providing reaches you directly—not an agency, attorney, or adoption consultant. You can also include a reassuring comment such as, "We're easy to talk to" or "We'd love to talk soon."

Here are a few things to consider when writing your ad:

- Unless you are in your early thirties or younger, avoid describing yourself as "young." It is quite possible that the expectant mother's mother is your age, which might not meet her definition of young!
- Avoid using references to God or religion.
- Do not specify the race or gender of the baby you are hoping to adopt. These delicate issues are best addressed at a later stage.
- Do not list your degrees, achievements, or titles.
- Do not comment on your income level or socioeconomic status. At the very most, simply state that you are "financially stable."
- Do not include any statement referring to payments or the exchange of money of any kind. An attorney or other qualified adoption professional should only address these issues.

- Consider writing both a long and a short version of your ad and determine which one to use based on the cost. Most papers have a set price for ads up to a certain number of words. If a particular paper is less expensive or doesn't limit words, you might want to take the opportunity to use a longer ad.
- To find papers to advertise in, first decide which geographic area you would like to target. Make certain that classified advertising is legal in that state by checking with your attorney or home study agency. (Laws change regularly, so be cautious about Internet searches that may produce out-of-date websites.) You may want to begin your campaign close to home, or at least in your own state, making an in-person meeting easier.
- Check a newspaper's website to find information on circulation (the larger the circulation, the higher the cost of advertising, but you'll get larger exposure), the days of publication, deadlines, and cost. I don't recommend that you place your ad directly through a paper's website. Given a choice, you will be more likely to get personal service and possibly a more attractive ad if you talk to a salesperson directly.
- Print ads are much more expensive than Internet marketing. You could easily spend thousands of dollars before you realize it. I suggest that you set a monthly advertising budget and then choose a mix of large and small papers to spend the amount on each month. If you are placing ads in multiple papers, spread your ads out over the course of a month so you have at least one running all the time. By placing your ads at different times, it will be easier to stop advertising when you connect with an expectant mother and avoid paying for ads you won't need.

You will want to have a system in place to track your ad placement and the results each month. The best way I've found to do this is to create a simple spreadsheet with several columns across the top listing the information pertinent to your advertising efforts. Include the name and location of the paper, phone and fax numbers, dates of publication, deadlines, costs and notes about any particular requirements a paper may have (like word count), or the name of a particularly helpful sales representative. If you need to use a particular newspaper again later, you will have everything on hand to streamline your process.

When you call a paper to place your ad, ask the sales department for their best pricing and adjust your word count if necessary. Fax or e-mail your ad copy rather than trying to dictate the wording of your ad over the phone, which will reduce the likelihood of errors.

Finally, always ask the newspaper to send you a tear sheet of your ad, which is a copy of your actual ad as it appeared in the paper. Check your ad's text for accuracy and how it stands out on the page. If there is a typographical error in your ad, you can ask to have it corrected, and often the paper will run it again in the next publication free of charge.

13

Putting Your Mouth
Where Your Money Is

Throughout this book, I use terminology to describe adoption in a positive light. You should begin to learn and use positive adoption language now, so when you are an adoptive parent, your child will always relate adoption in a positive manner. Also, during your search for an expectant mother, you do not want to offend or turn off anyone by the language you use.

USING POSITIVE ADOPTION LANGUAGE

If you refer to a child's birthmother as the "real" mother, then what does that make the adoptive mother? A child thinks of their "real" mother as the woman they run to when they need a Band-Aid. Words not only have meaning, but they also evoke emotion. You may think your friends and family won't even notice, but you might be surprised at how quickly the people around you will pick up on the new words you use and start using them too. Most people don't use antiquated terminology to be offensive; they just don't know a better way. For example, the phrase "gave up for adoption" is extremely common, but conveys a negative impression of a birthmother who just "gave up her child" versus one who "made an adoption plan for her baby."

Teaching your friends and family how to talk about adoption framed in a positive light will make them feel more at ease when discussing the topic with you and gives you the chance to practice talking about it as well. Routinely using positive adoption language will give you greater confidence in your marketing efforts and help you feel better equipped to talk to adoption professionals as well.

Rather than saying:	Instead Say:
Birthmother (prior to an adoption)	Expectant mother
Real Mother/Father	Birthmother/Birthfather or First-mother/First-father
Natural Mother/Father	Biological Mother/Father
Children of your own	Children by birth or children by adoption
Gave up for adoption or put up for adoption	Made an adoption plan or placed for adoption
Keep your baby	Parent your baby
Adoptee	An adopted person

Interestingly, even before I knew anything about positive adoption language, I never used the words "I gave up my baby for adoption." I didn't feel comfortable with saying that. Instead I said something like, "I placed my son for adoption" or "My son lives with his adoptive family." I won't say this was a conscious decision, but saying that I "gave up my baby" just didn't fit how I felt about my adoption. To me, it implies that I had no choice or control over my decision, or that I just shrugged my shoulders and let whatever happened happen.

After working so hard to feel empowered in my own life, and now doing my best to help empower others, the phrase "gave up her baby" more than any other still makes me cringe whenever I hear someone use it. I find the phrase somewhat offensive, in the same way an adoptive mother would find the question, "Do you have any children of your own?" offensive, because apparently the child you already have who kept you up all night for the last two months doesn't really count!

TELEPHONE TUTORIAL

I recommend that you get a separate toll-free number just for the purpose of your adoption. Having an "800" number will enable anyone to call you, and you won't need to provide a specific area code. There are a few ways to accomplish this, but one relatively new option involves using a third-party company that is different from your current phone carrier. The company can provide you with your own toll-free number that rings on any existing line. Usually the company charges a small monthly fee plus the cost of a few cents per minute, so you really only pay for what you actually use. You can terminate the service or change your number at any time, and you can switch the line where the number rings as well. Many people use an existing cell phone line to add to their toll-free line and then just carry it with them at all times (this is what I affectionately refer to as a family's "bat phone"). Ask for a telephone number that begins with the prefix "800," since not everyone will know that a number beginning with another prefix (888, 877, 866, etc.) is also a toll-free call. Regardless of the prefix, include the words "toll-free number" when listing it on your profile letters, print ads, or business cards.

Obviously, you will want to answer your incoming calls whenever possible, but you should set up a voice-mail box specifically for your adoption for when you can't. Here are some tips for setting up your voice-mail box message.

■ When you are a married couple, the wife should record the

message. Since it is more likely that a woman will be calling you, a voice-mail recording in a female voice is more likely to encourage her to listen to your whole message.

■ Use an upbeat voice; try to avoid sounding too businesslike or monotone.

■ Immediately introduce yourselves with your first names and identify the number as your adoption line. For example: "Hi! This is Sarah and Jim, and you have reached our adoption line." This way the caller knows she has the right number and that you are expecting calls about adoption on this line.

■ Express that you're happy she called, disappointed you missed her call, and provide a specific way to best reconnect with her. If you are often unable to take calls during working hours, let her know that you always answer the line personally in the evenings if she would like to call then. If she would prefer to leave you her number, tell her you will call her back right away.

■ Wrap up by telling her that you are looking forward to talking to her or excited to talk soon, or some similar warm and inviting sentiment.

Here's an example of a good message: "Hi! This is Jill and Jack, and you've reached our adoption line. We are so happy that you called and so sorry that we couldn't answer just now. If you would like to call back, we are most likely to answer any evening after five PM. Or if you'd like to leave your number, we will definitely call you back right away. We hope we get to talk soon! Thanks!"

Once a month (or more if you'd like), call yourself on your toll-free number to check that the line is working the way it should! Ask someone you know living out of state to call it too. There is nothing more frustrating than spending hundreds of dollars on advertising, go weeks wondering why no one is calling, and then realize your phone line is malfunctioning!

E-MAIL

Even though you probably already have an e-mail account, I suggest that you also create a new e-mail address for this process. Consider using a name that is easy for people to remember (try to avoid random number combinations or clever misspellings); you might even want to find something that is reflective of your adoption. Something generic like mailto:sarahandjim@e-mail.com may not be available, but you may be able to get mailto:sarahandjimadopting ababy@e-mail.com. Don't use your employers' Internet address, even if that is what you use for your personal e-mail and are allowed to have multiple accounts. Numerous free e-mail services exist. To keep it simple, use this one address for all your adoption-related correspondence.

TAKING THAT FIRST CALL
(BREEEEAAATHE!)

Don't let the fear of talking directly to expectant mothers deter you from taking on this process. Remember, there is no one better to represent you than you, and I promise that the person on the other end of the line is just as nervous as you! You might find it useful to write down some of the helpful hints I'll cover in this section and keep them by the phone, so when you do get a call, you have a little "cheat sheet" to help you along.

For the same reason that you should have a female voice on your voice-mail message, it is best for the prospective adoptive mom to answer the phone. An expectant mother is more likely to hang up on a man, even if that man is the prospective adoptive father. If your only choices are for the call to go to voice-mail or have the prospective adoptive father answer, I still think a real person (yes, even a man) is the better option. Just be sure to follow these guidelines:

Answer with a friendly, "Hello, this is [your first name]!" This will immediately put the caller at ease because she will know by your name that she reached the right number. Don't just answer "Hello" because the caller may think she has the wrong number.

In every phone call you receive, the most important piece of advice I can give you is this: *your only goal for an initial phone call is to establish some kind of rapport!* That's all. Do not ask her a checklist of questions or explain to her the entire adoption legal process, and do not feel that she must tell you her entire life story! The absolute best thing you can accomplish in a first call is simply to make some kind of personal connection with her. If you hang up and realize after a thirty-minute conversation you still have more questions than answers, as odd as this may seem, I say great! A call that makes a personal connection is the kind most likely to turn into an adoption.

Break the ice by asking if she saw your ad (website, letter, card on a bulletin board, or whatever other marketing you are currently doing). When she says yes, sound happy and excited that your marketing efforts are working and ask her where exactly she saw your information. "Oh that's great! What paper did you see our ad in?" or "Where on the Internet did you read our profile?" A paper name might give you a clue about where she lives, but you might still have to ask. "Where are you calling from?" or "Oh, the *Topeka Star*—is that where you live?"

Next, ask this exact question to direct your conversation: "Are you considering placing your child for adoption?" The wording of this question is important, because her answer will quickly identify who she is and why she is calling. On many occasions, the call may not be from the expectant mother. It may be a friend or the mother of the expectant mother who is calling, or it may be someone who is wondering if you are interested in surrogacy or if you would consider an adoption from Eastern Europe. You might even get a call from other adoptive parents who saw your ad and just wanted to wish you luck or give you advice. Whatever the reason for the call, asking this very specific question should get you a direct answer.

If the caller indicates she is calling about adoption for her baby, a natural next question would be to *ask her how far along she is or her due date*. This question will also clarify if she is indeed pregnant, or if she is calling about a child already born.

If the caller is a male, don't immediately assume that it is a fake call, but proceed as you would with any other call. He might be calling because he is considering placing his child for adoption or he just might be the expectant father. *If the person calling claims to be an intermediary (friend, mother, boyfriend, birthfather, etc.), proceed as usual, but be sure to offer an invitation to talk to the expectant mother personally.* Don't send your profile unless you either talk to the expectant mother directly or have a clear indication the call is legitimate. For example, if the caller identifies himself as the boyfriend and you can hear a girl talking in the background, answering questions or interjecting information for him to tell you, it is probably safe to assume he is telling the truth.

After you've established who's calling and why, you want to drive the conversation in a positive direction. Instead of asking, "Why are you considering adoption?" ask "Have you been thinking about adoption for a long time?" The first question could easily be interpreted as "What's wrong in your life that you aren't going to parent your baby?" making her feel that she must then list all the negative factors that led her to this decision.

Rather than asking, "Have you been seeing a doctor regularly?" you could say, "How have you been feeling during the pregnancy?" The latter question communicates that you care, not just about the baby's health, but about her as well. Most of the time, asking her how she has been feeling leads her to offer information about her prenatal care and her baby's health as well. Ironically, each of the two different questions leads to the same revelations, but asking the second version frames your inquiry in a much more positive and less scrutinizing way.

Ask her if she has any specific questions about you, or would she just like you to give her a little background. She may be a talkative person and the conversation might naturally take off, but then again, it might not. By the way, it really is okay to tell her that you are so nervous, you think you might faint. I promise, she will relate to it!

Talk about the topics that you have in your profile, basic facts as well as more specific details: hobbies, interests, why you are adopting, and so on. Try to avoid the things that could point out your obvious differences, such as age, religion, race, and so on. If she asks you any specific questions about these things, always answer truthfully! Then reflect the question back to her in a way that will help you understand why she asked it. For example, if she asks you what religion you are, you could answer like this, "We are a Jewish family. Is religion something that is important to you in a family?" This will not only help you discover if this is a good "match," but also give her an easy way to let you know if you really aren't the perfect family for her baby.

If a question concerning race comes up, the most important thing you can do is to answer the question honestly. This issue can come up in different ways; she may just come out and ask if it is okay with you that her baby is "mixed," or she might ask if you are only looking for a white baby. If the race of the expectant mom's baby is anything other than what you are prepared to adopt, I urge you to tailor your response based on this belief: for every infant adoption, there is a perfect family, and in some cases that family just isn't you. In other words, there is nothing wrong with her baby; her baby is perfect; but on the other hand, there is something wrong with you—nothing personal, but you simply aren't the perfect family for her baby.

It is even okay to apologize to her, "Oh, I'm so sorry, it sounds like we aren't the right family for your baby; I wish we were. Maybe you can call an adoption professional in your area who could help you find the perfect family. Don't stop looking, because they're out there somewhere!"

If a caller asks about money or about any kind of financial assistance, refer to the advice of an attorney or professional. Here is the best response to questions about money (you may even want to memorize it): "We are happy to help in any way that's legally possible."

It is essential that you leave financial discussions and arrangements to someone qualified to handle them. This is for your own legal as well as emotional protection. Sometimes financial need comes up as a very natural and legitimate part of the conversation. The expectant mother may not have insurance and is wondering about medical bills, or she may be worried about paying the rent while she is unable to work for six weeks postbirth—all things understandably concerning to someone in her shoes. Again, you can reassure her that you are certainly willing to help in any way that's legal, and since you don't know what legal is, you will need to get professional help from someone who does.

If the person calling is facing an immediate crisis and is asking for immediate financial help, you can offer to help her locate a social service agency or shelter in her area, but that is really all you should ever do. It can be very hard to resist the urge to want to immediately help in a case like this, especially if she says she is pregnant, living in her car, and wants you to adopt her baby, which will be born any minute!

No, I am not cold or callous to the fact that people face real crises and may really need help, but consider the following: Know, first, that some callers do not tell the truth; some may not be pregnant at all, some are desperate for money, and others deliberately deceive you because they know that if a couple wants a baby bad enough, they will often do just about anything to get one.

When I worked for an agency, families would frequently contact us, begging us to respond quickly to an expectant mother in crisis so they would not lose a valuable lead. More times than I can count, the "expectant mother" provided a fake address or she never showed up at the restaurant where we were supposed to meet, or she would not pick up her cell phone. Whether it was the threat of her fraud being uncovered by a legitimate authority or because she found another solution to her crisis, I never knew, but I was sure that adoption was not her real aim.

Even if an expectant mother calls with a true financial crisis, remember: you are not a social service agency and certainly not equipped to provide the kind of help that truly makes a long-term difference. You must keep a clear head and remember that your goal is to connect with a woman who is hoping to connect with you for the sole purpose of making an adoption plan for her baby.

Okay, even if you disagree with my previous advice, be fore-warned: *Never ever—under any circumstances—give money directly to an expectant parent.* With only very rare exceptions (when instructed by an attorney or qualified professional), all monies and/or expenses paid by adoptive parents must go through a qualified intermediary to avoid any risk of legal problems later. Aside from making your adoption legally sound, following this simple rule will help you avoid nearly every scam possible.

If any other questions come up that either you don't know the answer to or are better left to a professional, it is perfectly okay to admit that you don't know the answer, but that you will certainly find a professional who will. Even when you know the answer, if it is a legal question or adoption policy question, it is usually wise to check with an attorney or adoption professional.

When the conversation begins to wind down, end the call by ask-ing if you may send her a copy of your paper or video profile. Ask for her physical address (not only a post office box) and let her know how and when she can expect the letter to arrive. In Chapter 10 we discussed renting a mailbox in a retail location to use as a return address. Make sure to use that return address on these envelopes rather than your personal address.

The faster an expectant mom receives your letter the better, so send the package overnight, or at least use a form of delivery that can be tracked. Even if she's looked at your profile online, you still should send her a paper copy. This serves two purposes: it allows you to get a physical address (which can then be confirmed) and reach out by including a short, handwritten note telling her how much you enjoyed your conversation. *Be sure to offer her the opportunity to call again.* This final gesture puts the decision to move forward entirely in her hands. Track your letter to be sure it is delivered, and then wait. Do not call her again.

In the rare case that she declines your offer of mail because of a confidentiality concern, you can offer to send the letter in a plain white envelope, rather than overnight delivery, with nothing written that may identify it as adoption-related. I have also had families use a code word or phrase that the expectant mother chooses as part of the return address. The expectant mother may be worried that a letter from an unknown address will attract suspicion from someone else in her household.

FAKE CALLERS

Be prepared to encounter fake callers. Most often these callers are harmless and are lonely people seeking attention. My advice is to turn off your phone at a reasonable time each night and go to bed, since good calls generally come during the waking hours. If you are advertising in a different time zone, you can certainly take that into consideration, but do not feel you must sleep with your phone under your pillow just in case the perfect call comes in at two in the morning!

Sometimes a caller will provide you with a made-up address at the end of the first conversation or simply hang up without giving you any address at all. Since you can never really be sure about a caller, you should treat every call as if it is genuine. Even if you are completely suspicious, don't let on—you might just be wrong.

Fake calls frequently come in around the holidays. Remember that you have complete control in every situation and always have the power to simply hang up, which is exactly what I recommend you do in any situation where you begin to feel uncomfortable or when anything inappropriate is said. If you were able to obtain the caller's number on your caller ID, you can block it forever or simply don't answer any other calls from that number. You might be surprised, but some fake callers have been doing this as a sort of hobby for years!

Finally, always remember that the fake callers are not birthparents, so be careful not to let them color your feelings about the women who really are.

14

Intermatchment:
The Steps In Between

FIGURING OUT THE NEXT STEP

Good calls often move forward to the next stage quickly. If an expectant mom calls back shortly after receiving your paper profile or video, you need to decide what next step makes the most sense. If you are connecting with an expectant mother through a network of friends or family, you probably won't hesitate to move forward to a personal meeting right away. If you are moving forward with a lead from an ad or the Internet, your next move depends on a couple of factors.

If the expectant mom lives within driving distance and says she'd like to meet you, then offer to meet her for lunch or dinner. Let her know that she is welcome to bring a friend or family member along for support. Set the date for as soon as possible, not letting too much time pass.

If the expectant mother is in another state or lives too far away to drive to in a reasonable amount of time, you will have to make a judgment call. There is no right or wrong way to proceed in this situation, but based on a number of factors (described below), you may decide that you want to travel to meet her in person before involving anyone else, or you may want to contract with a local adoption resource to meet with her before you meet her yourself.

Some of the factors that may influence your decision include her due date (if she is due quite soon, she may feel more anxious to have her plan established), her preferences (does she ask a lot of questions that you don't know the answers to, or does she seem hesitant to want to talk to outside professionals?), how complicated the situation seems (is the birthfather around, involved, cooperative?), and last, what is your gut feeling? If you are having any nagging feelings of hesitation, find out if she is willing to meet with a professional—her openness may be a good indicator of her intentions.

If you choose to involve a professional first, explain to the expectant mother how it will benefit her. The professional will ensure the expectant mother knows her rights and choices and gets her what she needs through the process. Be careful not to suggest that you are having the expectant mother "investigated" before you are willing to meet her. In fact, you can certainly decide on a date to meet in the future at the same time you arrange for her to meet with the professional.

Keep in mind our discussions in earlier chapters about avoiding using the word "agency" when talking with expectant mothers; also avoid the word "counseling." Rather, use the term "advocate" or "adoption professional."

FACE-TO-FACE FOR THE FIRST TIME

Meeting a potential birthmother is certainly stressful. It might feel a little like a high-stakes interview, an intense exercise in compatibility matching, or a two-year courtship followed by an engagement all in one night! Since there doesn't seem to be any good name for this period of time, you probably already noticed that I took the liberty to make one up. I call this strange, awkward period "intermatchment."

If you are traveling a distance to meet each other, it will probably take some time to make those arrangements. In the interim, make at least one telephone call to the expectant mother to confirm your travel dates, and also to reduce some of the anxiety that comes with waiting.

Once a meeting is a go, remember that she really is as nervous as you are. Bring some photos or scrapbooks of yourselves and your family, which can be useful to help strike up some additional conversation. Dress casual and be yourself! Some expectant moms (and dads) bring along a list of questions prepared in advance to ask you. I've heard questions about everything from the seemingly unimportant, like, "What color is the baby's nursery going to be?" to "How do you plan to discipline?" Think of questions to ask her beyond the scope of her current situation, like what hobbies she enjoys, her favorite color, food, movie, and so on.

The feeling described over and over by people during a successful intermatchment is that it is so much more than merely checking requirements off a list—it is a deep connection that results from something you can't quite put your finger on, but you just click. It isn't uncommon for me to hear that people closed the restaurant on the night of that first meeting. On the other hand, don't worry if that doesn't happen to you; it doesn't necessarily mean that the connection won't go anywhere—just wait and see where it leads.

After your meeting, send the expectant mother a note or an e-mail telling her how much you enjoyed the time you spent together, and again, put the ball firmly in her court by asking her to call if she would like to talk again. This gives her the option of moving the relationship forward and simply gives her an easy "out." If she doesn't call or make contact, don't pursue her. If she decided you weren't the right family for her baby, she might feel awkward talking about it. If you thought the meeting was spectacular and you are just shocked she didn't call, reach out once. If you don't hear from her, it wasn't meant to be.

GETTING THE THUMBS-UP

Many expectant mothers make it a point to let a family know that she has specifically "chosen them." Sometimes they make this declaration before the end of the first meeting; sometimes it takes a little longer. Once you know that she has decided to stop her search for a family, you should also stop your marketing efforts.

If you happen to be one of those families who find themselves with more than one situation developing at the same time, you will most likely need to decide which one to pursue. Most people are able to make this decision based on some logical rationale, for instance, they met one expectant mom before meeting the other, or because they have already formed a strong connection with one.

Some families want to pursue two adoptions at once, which can be complicated. First, it is extremely important that you tell each expectant mother about your plan. If either is not in favor of your plan, I strongly recommend you don't continue. Since adoption is a sacred trust, I am sure you can see how important it is to be honest!

The other issues you may encounter relate to timing, logistics, and paperwork. A home study must be updated before every additional adoption can occur, and some agencies will not agree to update a home study soon after an adoption. Some agencies have a policy against anyone adopting twice in "less time than God intended" or because they oppose the practice of "artificial twinning," or adopting two biologically unrelated children of the same age. Not every agency imposes this kind of policy (in fact, if everything worked perfectly as "God intended," wouldn't we all be reading something else right now?), and some are willing to update your home study, in theory, at least.

WAITING . . . THE REAL LABOR

Once you've made a connection with an expectant mother and have identified the professionals you'll need (remember what we discussed in Chapter 9), the waiting period until the birth or the "intermatchment relationship," looks a little bit different in every situation. Some families talk on the phone to the expectant mother every day. Some families go to doctor appointments and ultrasounds or meet other members of the expectant mother's family. The most important thing you can do during this time is to give the expectant mother a chance to get to know you as real people. The more she feels she knows you, the more sure she will feel about her decision after her baby is born.

It's not easy to balance your excitement while at the same time protecting yourself from possible disappointment. If you have had other adoption connections that didn't work out, you might be afraid to let yourself get too emotionally involved again. This is something you don't have to hide from an expectant mother. Many expectant mothers wondered aloud to me if maybe they were the cause of the adoptive family's extreme nervousness. After giving them some insight into a family's past failed adoptions, they better understood the anxiety they sensed and were able to see the couple as just normal, scared people.

During intermatchment, continue to get feedback from the professionals helping you with your adoption. Sometimes situations change and circumstances develop that reshape your expectations for the adoption. For example, if the expectant mother had not yet shared her adoption plans with certain members of her family, their reaction could influence the adoption in either a positive or a negative way. (We'll talk more about red flags in Chapter 17.)

Try to see this time as an important opportunity—not only to lay the groundwork for a relationship with your child's birthparent, but also as an important chapter in your child's story that you will want to share with him or her someday. You might want to keep a journal, because believe it or not, as vivid as the experience seems now, there will be a day when many of your thoughts and feelings will fade. I kept a journal throughout my pregnancy with Grey, and every time I read it, I am struck by the acute intensity of my writing. Not to belittle that time, but I'm not sure I would remember too much of my day-to-day feelings during those months if I didn't have my own written words to remind me.

Building a relationship among the adults is much less complicated before a baby is born. After making my adoption plan and getting to know Ron and Sybil, I distinctly remember thinking, *This really sucks. I love this couple, and soon this baby is going to come along and mess up the whole friendship!* I had these thoughts because I wasn't planning on seeing Ron and Sybil after Grey's placement (our open adoption came along later), and I was truly enjoying having them in my life. Keep in mind, this was even before I had a clue about all the complicated emotions that come with giving birth!

Like any pregnant woman, I was incredibly sick of having a backache and swollen feet, and I was anxious to get the whole event over with. I spent a great deal of time talking to Ron and Sybil, and they spent many hours just listening to my hormonal babble! We orchestrated a plan for Grey's birth—I wanted them to both be in the delivery room, not as much for me as for Grey. I felt strongly that Grey's parents needed to be able to tell him that they loved him from the very moment he was born, to be the very first to hold him and begin caring for him right away. I wanted it all to feel normal for Grey. I neglected to consider one important detail—you know, the detail that there was another woman there, just slightly involved in the process too—yeah, that's her (*me*), the one who just gave birth. As misguided as this was, I guess my heart was in the right place; I just wanted my son to feel normal and loved, like any well-adjusted, nonadopted child.

It is important to talk together about everyone's expectations for the birth and for the time spent in the hospital. The best plan when it comes to this is to plan on the plan changing! Rarely does a hospital stay go exactly as you thought it would, especially if this is an expectant mom's first birth.

I have always felt that it is really unfair to ask an expectant mom to commit to major decisions, such as whether or not she would like to spend time with her baby at the hospital or what kind of post-placement contact she would like later, when she has no idea what it feels like to give birth. She may feel confident making these decisions before she gives birth, but after experiencing it, her feelings may change.

Any discussions you have with the expectant mother during intermatchment about future contact or long-term plans should be made with the caveat to revisit the topic again after the baby is born. Let the expectant mother know that it is really okay if she feels differently then.

Part IV

No, This Isn't Baseball
(As You Can See from All the Crying)

15

Keep Your Head and Hands Inside the Car at All Times— It Might Be a Bumpy Ride!

An expectant mother's hospital experience plays a pivotal role in her adoption. After giving birth myself, walking alongside other birthmothers in a professional role, and then listening to fellow birthmothers relive their own journeys, I know without a doubt that the hospital experience has a disproportionate amount of influence over the coloring of the birthmother's entire adoption experience. Little else has the potential to shape a birthmother's adoption story as much as what happens during the few days after her baby's birth. (So, hey, no pressure, parents!)

POLICY FOR "NORMAL PEOPLE"

When I arrived in labor at the hospital with Ron and Sybil, we were undeterred by both the staff's obvious skepticism of our unorthodox plan, as well as their crazy penchant for following the rules—especially the rule that said I was allowed only one coach in the labor room with me. Are you joking? After we had hauled our huge pillows (not to mention my huge ass!) to Lamaze class every week, for eight weeks, to hone our baby-birthing skills, there was no way that I was going to do this without them both, even if that meant giving birth right there in the hall!

Finally, after what felt like an eternity of hospital corridor debate, the staff made an exception for us so we could—all three—go right on into the labor room and get down to business.

ADOPTION DISCRIMINATION?

That may have been my first experience with, at the very least, a lack of adoption sensitivity, but it wouldn't be my last. My friend Amelia tells the story of a nurse who came into her hospital room to offer her some advice following the birth of her daughter, Renee. The nurse confided that she, too, was a birthmother and went on to tell Amelia that her adoption was the biggest mistake she'd ever made, that she regrets it every day of her life, and that she felt strongly compelled to talk to Amelia before it was too late for her too. Amelia did follow through with her adoption plan, despite the earnest warning, and now has one of the most comfortable open adoption relationships I have ever seen.

Sometimes adoptive parents and birthmothers feel as if hospital social workers are anti-adoption. Part of a social worker's job in a hospital is to confirm that the new mother isn't pressured, coerced, or taken advantage of in anyway by the people arranging her adoption or by the prospective adoptive parents themselves. I came to appreciate hospital social workers who approached situations with a healthy dose of skepticism and asked hard questions. I also learned the importance of preparing expectant mothers to expect a line of questioning from a social worker that may feel accusatory. The truth is the social worker can be a great advocate for both the birthmother and the adoptive parents.

The hospital social worker is usually a good person to ask about any specific hospital procedures, such as the discharge process and filling out the birth certificate. Sometimes the professionals you are working with will play an intermediary role with the staff at the hospital, but don't expect them to be at the hospital for hours and hours.

It isn't always just birthparents who experience adoption bias either. Once, while in the process of discharging a baby from an affluent suburban hospital, the nursery nurse refused to even acknowledge the adopting couple standing next to me. She never once spoke to them directly, but instead gave me the instructions on how to care for this newborn baby! At first I didn't understand what was happening (although I did think it was a little odd when she began explaining to me how to care for this baby boy's newly circumcised penis), so when I asked if she wouldn't mind giving these instructions to the ones who really needed to know them—the two people standing next to me—she instead told us in a very matter-of-fact tone that she could not, because the baby was being discharged to the agency, not to "those people." So, as ridiculous as the situation was, the nurse continued to instruct me on how to care for and feed the baby, and then finished by asking me if I had bought any formula yet.

Thankfully, stories like these are becoming less common as hospitals become better educated on adoption issues. Most adoptive couples are treated with warmth and dignity by hospital staff, and the birthmother is often looked to first for what role she would like the family to play during those first few days. Some hospitals offer an available room for the family to have some privacy until the baby's discharge. Some, with the birthmother's permission, will give them an identification bracelet allowing them to come and go into the nursery as any other new parent. I hope you experience the latter. Unfortunately you probably can't do anything about a hospital's policies (or decision to or not to enforce a policy) but you can call in advance to find out what procedures a hospital has regarding an adoption. Usually the best place to begin with this inquiry is with the hospital social worker.

WELCOME TO THE WORLD, BABY GREY

My beautiful firstborn son finally entered the world after umpteen hours of labor and many hours of pushing, masterfully executed without an epidural (the first and last time I would ever make that silly mistake again!).

Ron and Sybil never left my side. Ron was the Lamaze king, hee-hee-heeing me through every last contraction, and Sybil rubbed my back until her hands cramped. This one day forged a titanium bond between us that no amount of time or weather will ever tarnish. Face it, after you've watched someone give birth, there really isn't a whole lot left in the "getting-to-know-you" department!

Ron turned on the video camera the very moment Grey safely arrived and began capturing the first minutes of his life. Eventually, he turned the camera toward me and asked in his comfortable Southern drawl, "So, tell me, *Jinnifer*, was it the worst pain you've ever felt?" Without pausing I calmly shot back, "Uh . . . yeah . . . So, tell me Ron, was it the grossest thing you've ever seen?"

I joke now, but I'm grateful to have those minutes on film, because I'm not sure how much I would remember otherwise. Sybil held Grey first, then Ron, then me, which had been our carefully constructed plan. Once in my arms, Grey immediately opened his eyes, looked up at me, and stopped crying. That was the exact moment when the world stopped looking like anything I recognized as being familiar.

HEAD VERSUS HEART: REMAKING THE DECISION

Without a doubt, the most difficult time for everyone involved in an adoption is the short span of time between a baby's birth and when she must leave the hospital. These hours are so critical, because in order for any woman to follow through with her adoption plan, she must in some way remake her decision all over again. This is often her only real opportunity to be the sole mother to her child; even though she probably doesn't feel like the mother, she doesn't feel like a birthmother yet either. It is confusing, wonderful, and terrifying all at the same time.

I counsel expectant mothers to be aware of two different kinds of thinking that are going on all the time: head thinking and heart thinking. When a woman is pregnant, it is easy for her to think with her head and make logic-based decisions. This is when women will often make a list of "pros and cons" about parenting and can spout off a laundry list of things, tangible and intangible, that she would not be able to provide for her child. Head thinking always makes an adoption plan seem as clear as the Caribbean Sea. That all changes when she looks at her new baby and thinks, *Wow! I thought I knew what love was, but apparently I was seriously mistaken, because I have never loved anything like I now love this baby!* And that's when her heart takes over.

If you want to see an excellent example of this, the MTV television series *16 and Pregnant* episode where Catelynn gives birth to her daughter Carly captured it perfectly. Catelynn and her boyfriend, Tyler, had a mutually agreed-upon plan that they would not see or hold their daughter after she was born. They purposefully chose a couple to adopt who lived in another state because they thought they would not want their daughter close by and had decided on a semi-open adoption, one where photos and letters every so often would reassure them that their daughter was doing well.

Immediately upon Carly's entrance into the world, the obstetrician tried to persuade Catelynn and Tyler to take a first look at their new baby girl. Catelynn quite strongly said, "I don't want to see!" while Tyler hugged her tightly, also sobbing. Not long after the birth, Catelynn and Tyler discussed whether or not they should change their plan and spend some time with their daughter. Catelynn narrated that moment by saying, "Even though I said that Brandon and Theresa could hold her right away, I wanted to be the first to hold her." The camera captures perfectly what I know, first-hand, to be a defining moment in Catelynn's young life. As her baby is placed into her arms, the head thinking is completely over-whelmed by the huge swell of heart-thinking emotions.

The circumstances that prompt any woman to make an adoption plan to begin with usually haven't changed, but once she sees her baby, they just don't seem as important anymore. In fact, nothing seems as important anymore. Even a woman who is already parent-ing other children can still fall into this trap. Ask any woman expecting her second child if she has some fears about whether or not she has the capacity to love her second child as deeply as she does the first. I have heard the sentiment, "I just didn't expect that I would love him in the same way." Somehow we manage to fool ourselves into thinking it will be different, but it never really is.

If an expectant mother is doing all of her thinking with her head while she is pregnant, it's important that she is reminded of her crit-ical job during the pregnancy. After all, if she isn't mothering her baby, then who is? Sometimes women don't realize that they should be nurturing their babies before they are even born. This kind of emotional connection before a baby is even born is a good thing for everyone. It means she is not only more likely to follow through with her adoption plan, but she is more likely to resolve her grief over the long term. It really boils down to this: you can't say good-bye if you never even said hello.

THE HOPEFUL, TERRIFIED, SOON-TO-BE ADOPTIVE PARENTS

This kind of emotional attachment is terrifying for adoptive parents to watch, not just because it is hard to see someone you care about feeling so sad, but also because the process of holding on in order to let go is quite counterintuitive. It feels much more comfortable when a women states, matter-of-factly at six months pregnant, that she already feels as if this is your baby. She may as well call herself an incubator, because she has no feelings at all. That is what really scares me.

MTV's Catelynn and Tyler episode of *16 and Pregnant* showed another perfect learning moment for anyone hoping to adopt: after deciding to spend time with their baby, Tyler, looking extremely shell-shocked, walks into a small room where the hopeful adoptive parents are anxiously waiting for news. Even though this young couple does a phenomenal job of remaining composed, it was obvious that no one had told them to expect this. Tyler lets them know that Carly has been born healthy and that she is in the nursery. After a small pause, he tells them that Catelynn "just wanted to see her real quick, uh, and just hold her and say whatever . . ."

Theresa, the soon-to-be-adoptive mom, interjects, nodding her head, "She does? . . . Okay." She takes a big, deep breath and nods some more. You can imagine the thought-bubble forming over her head that says, *She's seeing the baby . . . I knew this was going to happen; she's changing her mind . . .*

Tyler continues, "After that she kinda wants you guys to hold her then . . ."

Theresa makes a joke about them all crying and then asks Tyler, "Have you held her yet?"

"No, not yet."

"Are you going to?"

Tyler nods, "Yep . . . uh, yeah I am."

I give them a lot of credit. It could not have been easy to have a television camera recording what is, in the best of circumstances, the pivotal moment that adoptive parents both dream about and dread at the same time. I am certain that when the cameras left, Brandon took his wife in his strong arms and held her as she sobbed, terrified that they had come so far only to have it end so quickly. (I honestly don't know this for a fact, but I would love for them to let me know if I am indeed right!)

At the same time, I am somewhat bewildered that no one told them this would happen. I feel bad for any family who comes into a situation expecting one thing and then suddenly has everything shift, as the thing their hearts long for most hangs in the balance.

As a counselor, I would've taken one look at Catelynn and Tyler and immediately told this family to expect not only this hospital plan to change course, but their desires for more contact going forward as well. I am especially sure of this now that I have had the pleasure of getting to know Catelynn. She and Tyler did continue with their adoption plan and they do love the adoptive parents they chose for Carly. They also wish that she lived closer and that they had more contact than they originally thought they would want. It has been a tough road, but they are a remarkable young couple.

THE COUNSELING CONUNDRUM

This is one of the biggest dangers associated with expectant mothers receiving no counseling, inadequate counseling, or counseling that only addresses adoption as a legal process. A woman who has few emotions during her pregnancy is exactly the type of expectant mom who would benefit most from counseling but, ironically, is also the least likely to seek it.

In a field where professionals are underpaid and overworked, it is hard to find knowledgeable counselors. I counsel expectant moms to be prepared for their heads and their hearts to go to war with each other. This tug-of-war will cause them to swing back and forth a thousand times trying to decide what they should do. The new moms who are able to keep a reasonable balance between both kinds of thinking are the women who decide to continue with their adoption plans.

16

Weddings, Funerals, Baptisms, and Bar Mitzvahs—So Why Not Adoptions?

If I could make one single rule about adoption that everyone must obey, it would be that no birthmother (if she chooses, of course) be allowed to leave the hospital without her baby in her arms. It is an all-too-common theme for birthmothers: leaving the hospital without their baby is a memory that forever haunts them. There is already so much for a woman to process in such a short amount of time. In addition to the physical trauma of giving birth, she is exhausted, a hormonal train wreck, and is often asked to make medical decisions for a baby that she is not planning to parent. Many women say that the dread they felt about leaving began to grow the minute they entered the hospital's front doors.

As a woman who just gave birth, the physical act of leaving the hospital with empty arms is incredibly shameful. A hospital is a very public place; everyone in the lobby is staring at you (and if they're really not, you think they are). You can do little to hide the fact that you've been sobbing, and to top it off, it's obvious that you've just had a baby because you still look eight months pregnant. Then again, maybe it's the flowers and the "It's a Girl" balloon. People take one look at the balloon and your red, puffy face and quickly look away.

It isn't that great for the adoptive couples either, so I don't think I'm really taking anything away from their wonderful memories. Sometimes I, the social worker, was required to sit in the wheelchair and be pushed out of the hospital holding the baby, while the adoptive couple brought up the rear, feeling, I'm sure, more than a little foolish. In the case where the adoptive mom is allowed to carry her new baby out, I hardly think she's secretly fantasizing that she just gave birth, and it's only because she is so super-fly-fantastic that she is back into her size six jeans already! If anything, I know more new adoptive moms are wondering why, if this is the moment she has been waiting for, for so long, does she feel like she's stealing someone else's baby?

When birth and adoptive parents all walk through the hospital lobby together, which also happens frequently, it is still horrible when they get into separate cars and drive off in different directions. Honestly, I think those endings are the worst. The birthmother stands and watches as this wonderful family that she loves so dearly (yet is also insanely envious of at the same time), straps her tiny baby's car seat into their SUV, receives the biggest, most emotional hug of her life, and then watches her child's new family drive away. The scene closes with her watching them get smaller, and smaller, and smaller . . . until they finally disappear.

I know a time of real parting is inevitable, but I also know many birthmothers who still suffer from anxiety, even panic attacks, years later, when they walk into any hospital. My friend Laura recently shared how proud she felt that she had finally conquered the enormous anxiety she felt about returning to the hospital where her daughter was born. For two years she even drove extra miles to and from her office just to avoid seeing the building. I had no idea! If this is what happens to an incredibly smart, strong, professional woman, we must be terribly underestimating the trauma this experience can cause.

There are better ways. One obvious solution comes from recognizing the value we already place on using ritual, ceremony, and tradition to mark the significant events in our lives. We all regularly attend weddings, funerals, birthday parties, baptisms, graduations, and so on. Rituals serve many important purposes, but we probably take most of them for granted. So why do we even bother?

Imagine if a loved one died but there was no funeral. What if graduation was your high school sending you a diploma in the mail? What if you moved to another state but never said good-bye to any of your neighbors before leaving?

Ceremonies provide a framework for our grief and an opportunity to celebrate achievement and to connect with those we love surrounding important themes in our lives. They are socially established ways that tell us how to act in order to acknowledge a change, a transition, or a rite of passage—some happy and some sad. So why don't we include adoption in that list as well? Lois Ruskai Melina and Sharon Kaplan Roszia sum up the reasons very nicely in *The Open Adoption Experience*: "Rituals are needed in adoption because adoption creates new relationships and new family units. In open adoption, where the birthparents will remain involved with the child, the exchange of roles must be clearly understood by everyone. Furthermore, because adoption is often a bittersweet experience, rituals help people express their emotions and help them heal."

CHAMPAGNE AND ANGEL FOOD CAKE

After Miranda and Jon officially chose Frank and Karen, the two couples planned every aspect of the birth and adoption placement that they possibly could. Jon and Miranda were reluctant to accept any financial help from the family, but in the end, Miranda was placed on bed rest and Frank and Karen helped with the expenses that were allowed by law. They all went to a childbirth class together and told me that they felt this birth did not belong to them, but to their daughter, and that they should try to make her story as peaceful, for her sake, as it could possibly be.

This adoption was, and still is, the best representation of cooperative open adoption that I have ever been a part of. It certainly wasn't what most people do, nor would I recommend it for everyone, but it certainly worked beautifully for them. After little Stella was born, Miranda and Jon took her home with them to their tiny apartment for five days. Miranda breast-fed her, Jon changed diapers, and they took a thousand photos of them together in their little cocoon.

They talked to Frank and Karen on the phone every day, who could do little to hide their anxiety. Every day, upon my advice, they said the words, out loud, that they weren't changing their minds, that they were still committed to the adoption plan, and that if adoption stopped being the plan, they would call them right away. Everyone around Frank and Karen told them they were nuts. There was no way that this young couple could spend five days with their newborn baby and still "give her up." One friend said she couldn't believe they'd paid good money to an agency who'd allow such a thing!

Friday evening came, and as planned, Frank went to pick up Miranda, Jon, and Stella and bring them back to their house for a placement ceremony. Karen was too terrified to go with him, thinking that everyone in the entire world couldn't possibly be wrong, and that certainly Frank would get to Jon and Miranda's apartment to find the whole thing had been called off. I, too, had talked to Miranda and Jon every day and knew that they had absolutely not changed their minds. Being a young and inexperienced social worker, I was astonished that somehow it seemed the cocoon experiment had produced just the opposite effect of what everyone predicted. On Thursday evening, the last night that Miranda and Jon would spend with Stella, I went to visit them. They were appropriately exhausted (apparently Stella was a night owl like her birthfather), absolutely devastated at the thought of letting her go, and profoundly committed to doing just that. Jon said that having their time with Stella made them both realize not only how hard taking care of a baby really was, but that the only real way they could show their daughter how much they valued her was by giving her a life with Frank and Karen. They loved Frank and Karen, trusted them, and even talked about being excited to see how happy they would be when Stella was finally home sleeping in her new nursery. They were laughing and crying at the same time, feeling so bittersweet about the whole thing.

The entrustment ceremony was incredible. They planned everything together and asked if Frank and Karen's social worker, Carol, and I would be willing to come and facilitate. I, being new to the whole profession, had no idea just how remarkable it was. I certainly didn't realize how honored I should have felt to have been asked to be a part of it. It will always be on my list of highlights from this career.

Everything was captured on video so Stella could watch it someday too. At one point, Jon spoke to the camera as if he were speaking to Stella sometime in the future, telling her, "Don't give your parents too much trouble when you become a gorgeous young woman like your birthmother here." They had each written something for Stella and took turns reading aloud, talking about committing themselves to doing whatever was the best thing for her, no matter how hard.

When they requested that they sign the actual surrenders as part of the ceremony, I wasn't sure that it was a very good idea and tried to talk them out of it. They said that signing the papers wasn't the hard part for them; by the time they had gotten that far, they had already made the decision in their hearts, and the surrenders were just a piece of paper to them. We finally came to a compromise that satisfied everyone, including the agency and the attorney we asked for advice. While Miranda and Jon were completing the surrender papers, Frank and Karen left and walked down the block to a coffee shop. Carol stayed at the house with me and acted as a witness. I wanted to be sure that neither Miranda nor Jon felt any pressure to sign, and with the family gone, I could make it clear that they could take more time, they didn't have to sign surrenders at all, and that even at the very last moment, I would take them and Stella home in my car if they wanted to call the whole thing off. They didn't.

With the legal documents making it official, Frank and Karen entered their front door with uncertain looks on their faces. Miranda and Jon were standing with Stella in their arms and immediately walked over to them. Miranda gently placed Stella in Karen's arms, an intentional gesture that signaled the mother was now a birthmother, and that it was a choice freely made.

When we could finally catch our breath, the ceremony continued with two rituals, both intended to represent the concept that they all would have a role in Stella's life. Carol and I read a story about unity and family, while they passed a spool of ribbon around their little family circle until they were all enclosed and the ends tied together. The reading ended on the sentiment that members of a family are like the ribbon. Even though they are individuals and won't always be together (they proceeded to cut the ribbon into four equal parts), it was still easy to see that they all were, at one time, seamlessly joined, a fact that would never be diminished by the uncertainties of life.

The second ritual used four white stretched canvases that they placed on the floor. They then painted the bottom of Stella's feet with hot pink paint and carefully placed her footprints in the center of each canvas. Then the adults painted their hands with their own colors and placed their handprints in a circle around Stella's tiny feet. Before Stella's canvas was even fully dried, Frank hung it in her nursery above her crib.

As an appropriate ending to what now felt more like a celebration, Karen brought out champagne and pink angel food cake. She said this was the beginning of a new family tradition, and that they would celebrate Stella's "gottcha day" this way every year.

I certainly don't expect everyone to have such an elaborate plan, but any plan at all is better than leaving those moments to chance. If you are intentional about your adoption, it will be empowering regardless of how it's done. Even if you leave the hospital and go to the agency, to someone's home, or to a park, any kind of meaningful transition will help cushion your landing into your new roles.

One thing I insist upon in every adoption is to help everyone decide when, where, and what their first contact will be. This serves a dual purpose: it allows the adoptive parents to begin earning the birthmother's trust by making a promise and then keeping it, and it allows the birthmother to be unafraid to express what she needs in the coming days, reducing her anxiety around the question of "now what?" When this kind of planning doesn't happen, everyone goes home and then wonders what the next step should be. Everyone second-guesses their instincts and finally just decides it's safer to not risk bothering anyone. Besides, wouldn't they call if they wanted to talk anyway? Some women are not able to ask for what they need under ordinary circumstances, but when the stakes feel this high, it can require great reassurance from the adoptive parents to believe that their request is even worthy of being heard!

DAYS OF BITTERSWEET

After Grey's birth, I spent two weeks with him and his new family before getting on a plane to fly two thousand miles home. Honestly, this arrangement really didn't seem strange to us. I guess because no one ever warned us against it, we just never thought twice about it.

If you ask me, the very second you become a mother, regardless of how you become a mother, your brain surrenders, and those tough layers of your heart are peeled back to expose the most vulnerable, helpless part of your soul. Frankly, it wouldn't have been any easier or harder had I spent two minutes, two days, or two weeks with Grey after he was born. Babies are like the Borg, "Resistance is futile!"

I remember talking with Sybil late one night, as we often did, about why she gave me her full name and telephone number, even though she knew absolutely nothing about me. I wondered why, after talking with the awful agency that made me feel so criminal, her instincts seemed to be so completely opposite. She told me that in her mind, it seemed like she had no reason to not trust me, so why wouldn't she?

We sat quiet for a minute and stared at Grey, who was sleeping in his white bassinet between us. Sybil broke the silence and said simply, "Who makes these rules anyway?"

17

When She Becomes the Mom

I want to open this chapter by being very clear that I believe when an expectant mother changes her mind (or her heart) and decides to parent her baby, I do not consider the adoption plan to have been a failure. As strange as this may sound, I don't think you should either. She has every right to decide to parent if adoption isn't the best plan, and trust me, you will not feel good about adopting a baby whose birthmother was somehow talked into, coerced, or not given any option other than placing her child! With only a few exceptions, I generally walked away from these situations feeling that the right woman had become the parent.

WEATHERING A FALL-THROUGH

You must be prepared for the reality that not every adoption plan will become an actual adoption. If you experience a fall-through, that does not mean you've failed, and it is no reflection of your worthiness to become a parent. The adoption industry needs to quit measuring success only by the number of placements made in a year, but also by how few casualties they left in the wake of the placements they did complete.

I know it is easy for me to say, since I'm not the one who will be going through this! True, true, but don't forget that everyone in adoption has losses; no one signed up voluntarily for this trip, and the universe isn't just picking on you in particular!

If you have endured any kind of infertility, then you are already more than familiar with bracing yourself for loss. In some ways adoption is no different than infertility loss, yet in one very significant way, it couldn't be more different: with adoption, if you stick with this process, you will become a parent. That is something no infertility doctor can promise with any certainty.

You might already be more equipped to deal with an adoption fall-through than you think. Most couples figure out pretty quickly during the infertility routine that they didn't want to tell everyone everything every time they were waiting for test results. In that way, adoption is no different. Do tell everyone that you are hoping to adopt, but don't tell everyone every detail along the way. Good news is a pleasure to share, but bad news is never easy.

Here are two other important reasons. The news about infertility is pretty straightforward: you're either pregnant or you're not. No one usually wants to know what your HCG levels were or what injectable drug you will be trying next. Adoption is usually more complicated, and people do want to know what happened. Telling a story over and over again can be exhausting. It also doesn't help improve the less-than-great image domestic adoption is trying to shed either. People who were skeptical about your plans to adopt might now be thinking, *I told you so . . .*

The second reason to hold your cards close is because every adoption has a story, and every story is about a child, and that child is the rightful owner of his or her story. It should be up to that child, when he or she is old enough, to decide what, when, and with whom they share their story. This especially applies when the story contains sensitive information, and unfortunately, most adoptions do. Imagine if as you grew older, you realized that everyone around you already knew about the very terrible, tragic, and sad story that was the beginning of your life, and you were not the person who told them. I know there are many families who wished they had been given this advice before it was already too late.

When people ask, and they will, what is happening with your adoption, it really is acceptable to set some healthy boundaries for you and your family. A great answer might be, "Yep, we're still working on it," or "It's a slow process, but we're hanging in there." Remember, there is a big difference between privacy and secrecy.

If you do experience a fall-through, try to frame it as more of a "false start." That could be hard when you thought you were almost near the end of the process, but now you're right back to the beginning. Runners with a false start don't have to run nearly the whole race before going back to the line, but if that is what happens to you, try to see it as training. You will be much wiser your second time around the track! Take some time, heal together as a couple or family, and get back on the horse. It has been my experience that if people don't allow themselves to process a loss and instead lunge right into the next situation, those unresolved feelings can pop up and get in the way. At the same time, if people take too much time off, they begin to have fears that are much worse than reality. At some point, you gotta go Nike and "just do it."

WHAT IS THE MEASURE OF YOUR SUCCESS?

Measuring the percentage of women who decide to parent midway through an adoption plan is a very difficult number to calculate. What exactly determines a change of heart, a fall-through, a false start, or whatever other name you attach to it? If the baby is not yet born, does that count? Does the baby have to be in someone's arms or in someone's home, or is in your heart good enough for it to be considered a bona fide fall-through? Unless you are an organization who measures just to boast about your success rates, then the most practical way to measure a fall-through is to ask yourself, "Does this feel like a fall-through?" If you answer "yes," then it probably is.

Often situations fall apart for no apparent reason beyond circumstances that no one could have predicted or controlled. I have yet to meet a family who didn't think the ride was worthwhile after their adoption was complete, but I know that convincing them to "hang in there" during the process was sometimes a tough sell.

If you hold the belief that everyone gets the children they are meant to have, then you can understand how my former clients, Keri and Dan, could say that after almost three years of heartbreak, they understood exactly why it all happened to them.

Keri told me that, "If any of those other adoptions had worked out, then we wouldn't have Micah, and he's the one we were supposed to have." Keri laughs and says that if she had known she was starting the adoption process much sooner than they needed to, they would have slowed down a little! I would never have predicted that a couple like Keri and Dan would have such a rough road leading up to their adoption. They were wonderful and did everything "right," but they still encountered unpreventable events several times that landed them right back at square one. It was just rotten luck, really.

RECOGNIZING THE RED FLAGS

What makes a big difference in how a couple recovers after an adoption falls through is whether or not they saw it coming. Fortunately, most of the time, you will have seen the signs, and if things don't work out, you will not be completely shocked. When I think back over all the adoptions I've seen, I can only remember two cases in fifteen years when I, too, was caught completely off guard by a sudden change of heart.

The circumstances that lead a woman to parent are rarely as simple as her just "changing her mind." There are always complicating issues and other people with competing interests trying to influence her decisions. Women don't thoughtlessly set out to play pickle with some poor childless couple's dreams; on the contrary, the women I've known who changed their plan and decided to parent experienced tremendous guilt over the pain they knew their decision caused. Often there are signs to watch for and be aware of that commonly impact the outcome of an adoption.

THE NOT-SO-SUPPORTIVE FAMILY

Defying the wishes of your family is extremely hard, even if those relationships have not been very significant ones. It is one thing for a woman's family to mildly disagree with her plan, but some women receive tremendous amounts of direct pressure to parent. This can be especially true in certain cultures where adoption outside of the family is considered taboo. These families regularly come forward at the eleventh hour with promises of help and assistance, even though they are the same people who have never been there in the past. Nevertheless, if the promises come when she is most vulnerable, it is not hard to understand how she would allow herself to believe that things will be different this time, and that she really can parent after all.

Some families not only voice their disagreement, they may actively try to sabotage the adoption plan. One birthmother arrived at her mother's house during her seventh month of pregnancy to find that her mother had organized a surprise baby shower for her!

Some women's families offer what I call, "backhanded support." In other words, they say they will support you "no matter what you decide." These families usually mean well, but by saying they are in favor of any decision, they really affirm neither. If it is the birth grandmother who is offering this kind of support during the pregnancy, she often isn't prepared for the strong feelings that she, too, has for her grandchild, and whatever endorsement of the adoption plan she ever did give disintegrates quickly after the birth. The best kind of support for an expectant mom to have is someone, preferably family, who is truly behind her, reminding her that she is doing the right thing for the right reasons.

THE PRINCE CHARMING SYNDROME

An expectant mother who has been in a tumultuous relationship with the birthfather for any period of time faces a double dose of loss in an adoption: the loss of her baby and the loss of the relationship. The lack of a stable relationship is very often a key ingredient missing from the expectant mother's life, and she wants her child to have that stability. It is often listed as one of the primary reasons she considers adoption in the first place. Even when her relationship with the birthfather is seemingly over and she expresses great anger—even rage—toward him, it is only natural that she would still have mixed emotions for him after the birth. After all, the baby she just gave birth to is half his genes!

Some women are adamant that since he walked away when she needed him, she is not even going to call him to tell him his baby is born. Be prepared when after her baby arrives, and she is feeling that agonizing pull between her head and her heart, she may very well reach out to him anyway. Sometimes she is unconsciously holding on to one last shred of hope that if he would only see his child, he would come to his senses.

If this happens and he does step up (or if his mother steps in and offers to help), she may decide to parent her baby after all. I have seen this kind of scenario end in both ways, and in the case that he rides in to rescue her, no one was especially surprised by the sudden turn of events.

DENIAL (IT AIN'T JUST A RIVER IN EGYPT!)

We talked about this red flag a little bit in Chapter 15, but it is certainly worth mentioning again, because it is probably the most common reason I've seen for women's adoption plans to change. Denial, in healthy doses, is a valuable skill that can serve us well when we are in pain. I think of it as having the ability to take a break from whatever it is we are dealing with, much like how going to a funny movie can sometimes take your mind off things for a couple of hours. I often encourage women to take a break; it helps them develop the valuable skill of self-care, but when that break becomes a permanent way to put off the inevitable, it can be dangerous.

When an expectant mom is using a great amount of denial to cope with her fear and loss, it usually works pretty well while she is still pregnant, but too often those walls come crashing down after the baby (and reality) arrives. There are only so many emotions a person can deal with at once, and the quantity that are involved with an adoption quickly become too overwhelming for just about anybody to handle.

Often, women who claim they did not know they were pregnant until very late, or at all, might be telling the truth, not because their body wasn't giving them all the signs of pregnancy, but because they just didn't want to see them. Women who do denial really well usually learned this skill when they were very young and have it well honed. When an expectant mother is deeply in denial, often others in her family are too; after all, that is probably who modeled it so well for her to begin with! Don't underestimate how powerful denial can be.

Women in denial will often express having little or no emotional connection to their baby. They may tell you that they feel like the baby is already yours or that they are only growing this baby for you. They may not want to participate in any meaningful rituals like choosing names or talking about who the baby might look like. They may state that they don't even want to see the baby at all after the birth, fearing that this will trigger the demise of their defense system. Expectant mothers in deep denial are less likely to take good care of their babies prenatally. They may smoke cigarettes, drink alcohol, and not see a doctor regularly, because they do not allow themselves to think about the harm they could be doing, and they may not be aware of their body's signals of medical problems.

The kinds of behavior I am referring to here do not concern women who have a serious addiction (although denial is definitely an element in that too); rather, I am talking about someone who has an occasional beer or smokes some recreational marijuana and then later often feels great remorse and regret about her actions.

The best thing you can do when your child's expectant mother is using strong denial to cope is to continually reassure her that it is okay for her to love her baby, that her child will always know she loves him or her, and that her child will not grow up to hate her because of her adoption plan. Affirm her positive choices, like seeing a doctor or taking prenatal vitamins. Let her know that you love her too, not just her baby, and that you are grateful she is such a good mother to her baby during the pregnancy.

Communicate often that whatever the plan for the hospital or her wishes for post-placement contact are now, it is also okay if her wishes change after the baby is born. I know it happens, but I personally have never had even one birthmother who said she did not want to see her baby in the hospital, who did not then feel differently when the actual time came. In the one instance when the birthmom did leave the hospital without seeing her baby, she called me the next day asking if I would bring her daughter over before she signed any papers.

Don't assume any agreement you've made about post-placement contact before the birth is a settled issue. Even if the counselor working with the expectant mother tells you it is all settled, don't be so sure. It is not a fair expectation that a women will know what she would like or need until after that baby is really real. I completely disagree with any agency or counselor who regularly completes any kind of verbal or written agreement (even if not legally binding) before the baby is born. For you, the adopting family, that practice also does a huge disservice. An expectant mom who says she only wants a few pictures and letters every year around their child's birthday may suddenly not be able to imagine life without seeing her child regularly. It happens all the time; the adopting family thinks they know what to expect, when suddenly the baby arrives and they are forced to think about a significantly different adoption than the one they thought they were signing up for. Of course, they agree to the new level of contact because they don't want to risk losing this opportunity to adopt, but later, the relationship is always under a tremendous amount of strain, which often never gets resolved, all because everyone's needs and wants were never honestly addressed in the first place. Families inadvertently break promises and birthmothers become resentful; for some families the stress in open adoptions overwhelms the potential benefits. Professionals must not be afraid to disappoint an adoptive family; adoptive families must be honest about what level of contact they are really willing to participate in, and birthmothers must be offered the opportunity to have more time to digest their new reality.

SAYING "YES" BUT MEANING "NO"

When an expectant mother's words and actions don't sync, there is usually more going on. It is not uncommon for someone who is having a change of heart to be afraid to tell you. Even though you are the first person who needs to know, you might be the last to find out. Depending on the woman's level of maturity, she may not tell you at all but just quit calling and disappear. She may send you a letter or tell the counselor who is working with her, who then calls you. You may never get any reason why, or any resolution in your own mind, about what happened.

If you have a gut feeling that something is up, listen to your instinct. If an expectant mom says she will call but then doesn't, suddenly stops answering her phone when you call, or has a laundry list of excuses of why you haven't heard from her when you do catch her on the phone, read between the lines and just stop pursuing her. Let her know you are here, put the ball in her court, and leave it be. If she knows how to reach you and your line is functional, there is probably nothing you will accomplish by calling more except to make yourself crazy!

If this happens, try not to invest a lot of emotional energy trying to figure out what happened, and don't let it taint your views of birthmothers. Obviously, if a woman is not mature enough to tell you that she is changing her plan, then she would not have been mature enough to complete an adoption plan either.

Part V
Unlike a Highway, a Pet, or a Tree, This Adoption Is Forever

18

Exhaustion: It's Nature *and* Nurture

Pinch you. Yes, you finally have what you've dreamed about for so many years. You are, at last, going to recoup some of the thousands of dollars in baby gifts you've bought for all your girlfriends over the years, and for once you can give someone else some words of warning about the perils of mommydom (even though you won't have access to the horror stories of cracked nipples, there is still plenty of other material left for you to use!), and soon, this tiny bobble-headed lump will look up at you, smile, and call you "Mama."

There is plenty of upside to adopting a newborn. If there is any truth at all to the nurture thing, you are going to get the full shot at it. I'm not afraid to say that there are times when I think I gave all my best "nature" genes to Grey—the sweetest, most generous boy you have ever met in your life—and the most exasperating genes to the boys I'm parenting! (I know, I know! Exasperating or not, at least I got to give it a try, something that I am sure Sybil still would have loved the opportunity to have!)

Ron and Sybil have a very unique situation. It's a little confusing, so I'll try to keep it simple. Both Sybil and Ron have an identical twin. Ron and Sybil were married, and then not long after, their twin siblings married each other as well. So that means they were identical twins married to identical twins. Sybil and Ron tried and tried to have kids with no luck. It seems that they have built-in nuclear-war-like birth control, and if either of them had married someone else, they probably could have had biological children.

Soon, Ron and Sybil's twins had a family: two boys. Here is the remarkable part: if Sybil and Ron were able to have biological children, their kids would have genetically been siblings (first cousins by relation but siblings by DNA), because their parents have identical genes (I know, read that again to let it sink in . . .).

These two boys look exactly alike, meaning it would be pretty darn safe to say that Sybil and Ron's kids would have looked just like them, too. Talk about having your infertility in your face all the time! That would have been tough.

Sybil has joked with me over the years that she thinks her kids are much cuter than the ones she would've given birth to, and she doesn't just have to speculate on that like most people! I, of course, asked her why she didn't just get drunk and sleep with Ron's twin. After all, they are exactly the same, so no one else would know the difference! Let's just say that Sybil is a little more easily embarrassed than I am, and I don't think she thought that was nearly as funny as Ron and I did.

Most parts of parenting a baby by birth or by adoption are no different. I'm quite sure that Jana Wolff was right when she wrote, "Adopted poop doesn't smell any different." Your friends may think you're at an advantage because you don't have any baby weight to lose or because your husband doesn't have to wait for your episiotomy stitches to heal, but honestly, people, what difference would it make anyway? When you are getting up every hour with a newborn baby, there ain't nothing going on in that bedroom except sleeping!

The parts that are different, though, are significant. This is true especially if no one tells you what they are. You can finally go to playgroup, but you leave just feeling bad again, because it's clear that if you don't breast-feed your baby, you're going to hell; and rather than letting yourself enjoy a little sweet revenge when the other moms look at your waistline, look at your newborn baby, and look back at your waistline with envy, you feel like a fraud. No one told you that when you look at this beautiful baby sleeping peacefully in his crib, you would feel enormous guilt. In adoption, you cannot deny that your joy exists only because of someone else's pain, and you would rather have to heal from the stitches of a hundred episiotomies than have to think of that every time you begin to let yourself feel happy.

When I got on that plane to fly home, my heart was in total agony, but my head managed to get me into my seat and made me stay there. My own driving-away memory was not of a car but of me walking down an airport ramp toward the tarmac. This was in the days before terrorism, when you could still have a decent airport good-bye, and Ron and Sybil came to my gate and waited with me until that very moment came. Sybil was holding Grey, all wrapped up in a white hand-knit blanket. I can still see them standing next to the wall made of glass just like it was yesterday. Sybil's memory of that moment must be the same as mine, except exactly the opposite.

I knew that making the right decision would be worth it in the end. I knew that Grey was right where he belonged, but that didn't change the fact that I still wished he was with me.

UNDERSTANDING A BIRTHMOTHER'S GRIEF

Birthmother grief is much the same as any other grief, except that it isn't socially sanctioned and no one knows what to do with you. When you have just experienced the transforming power of giving birth, but have no baby, it's as if your pregnancy didn't count. Most times it isn't acknowledged; you don't get to be included in the club that sits around and brags about the horrors of labor and delivery, and you definitely don't get to be a mess for more than two weeks—after all, you did bring this on yourself!

When someone dies, there are some basic things that everyone says and does to comfort the family; no one can fix the situation, but at least people know what is expected of them and they can try to provide comfort. When a birthmother grieves, the pain she feels is the same, except most times there are no rules of etiquette for others to go by, so she gets little comforting.

In my situation, I walked off the gangway in Michigan and was met by my mother and sisters. It was all I could do to hold back my sobs until after I had reached my mother's arms. I don't know what people must've thought of six grown women standing in a huddle in the airport sobbing, but that was exactly what we were doing. I don't think we had ever cried together before that day, and I know we haven't done it since. (Let's just say that showing feelings in my family was never a strongly encouraged activity.) I pulled the photos of my precious baby boy from my purse and we began passing them around right then and there. Somehow I pulled myself together so we could drive home to my parent's house, marking the beginning of the crazy charade game I would, eventually, get very good at playing.

I arrived home just in time for dinner, which included my five nephews, one niece, and my eighty-year-old grandmother. My grandmother was one of the people who had no clue that I'd had a baby. Apparently, she was one of many who'd been told that I was in Florida being a nanny for a nice family. (Not exactly a lie, I guess.)

Dinner was the typical nightmare that occurred regularly at my house while growing up. My little nephew had already eaten, which meant that he wasn't interested in sitting at the table with the rest of us, which also meant that a two-year-old was touching my father's stuff while the rest of us were eating. My father lost his temper and started screaming, which was followed by my sister screaming back and crying.

She grabbed her son and left the house as the rest of us just sat there and continued to pass the mashed potatoes around the six-ton elephant who had made himself comfortable in the middle of the table. This was exactly why Grey deserved so much more than I could have given him.

REPRESSED GRIEF

When everyone around you isn't at all comfortable with your pain, or don't even know that you were pregnant, it's easy for some women to simply set their grief on a shelf and dust around it. Some women don't grieve for years. In fact, we have had women come to our birthmother retreats and they are f-i-n-e during that first year. They show up because they want to share the joy of how wonderful their open adoption is and how fabulous this experience is for them. Year two, the cracks in the foundation begin to show. By year three there is usually a full-blown flood in the basement and everyone in her life wonders what the heck just happened, because they didn't even know they were living in a floodplain!

Another common scenario happens when a birthmother has wanted no contact with her child or her child's family for years, when suddenly something in her own life triggers the loss of her child and she begins to grieve. The adoptive family, now accustomed to having no contact, is more than caught off guard when their child's birthmother suddenly contacts the agency with a request that the family provide regular updates.

It is a hard place for both parties, and I have empathy for everyone involved. The family never agreed to anything other than what they have—a closed adoption for all practical purposes, which is exactly what their child's birthmother claimed she wanted. Well, yes, that is what she thought too, and at least until now, it worked pretty well for her. Sadly, no one warned either of them that delayed grief is something that is a fairly common occurrence.

THE (I MISS MY) BABY BLUES

The first few weeks after placement are extraordinarily hard. I got out of my parent's house as fast as I could and moved in with one of the few friends who knew about my having had Grey. She was student teaching and gone all day, so I just sat around the apartment, no job, no school; I felt like someone had mixed up all the letters on my compass. Everything I thought I wanted didn't feel even remotely significant anymore. I planned to take just one semester off college, my senior year, then go back and pick up right where I'd left off, as if nothing had happened. I didn't really realize that that's not exactly how it works.

There were days during that time when my heart would begin to succeed in convincing my head to just give in and go along with its ridiculous plan. Poor Sybil—I called her almost every day, most times sobbing. I just didn't know what to do with myself, and she was the only one who I thought could understand just how miserable I felt. I didn't want to make her feel bad or to scare her that I was changing my mind; in fact, I told her in almost every conversation that I wanted to, but that I wasn't going to!

In addition to missing Grey, I was also missing them. For so many weeks we had spent hours together, talking, bonding, and dreaming about this baby, and then right after the most amazing emotional pinnacle possible—Grey's birth—wham! They were gone.

It happens all the time: birthmothers secretly wish that the family they chose could adopt them right along with their baby! In some ways, Sybil and Ron had assumed a paternal role in my life, joking that they would need to approve any guy I wanted to marry or that Ron would come beat up anyone who would dare break my heart. They felt protective of me and that felt good. This was not what I was expecting either. Right up until Grey was born, I couldn't wait to get back to my "old life." Now I was realizing that my old life didn't exist anymore, at least not as I'd known it.

ENTITLEMENT

Professionals call the process that adoptive parents go though after bringing home their new baby "entitlement." This is really just a fancy name for the process of getting over feeling sad for your child's birthmother. I know there is more to it, but really, the way to measure emergence from the entitlement period is when an adoptive mother can look at her child and not think, "I'm the adoptive mother," but, "Wow, I'm his mother."

After I'd been home for a month, Sybil and Ron flew up with Grey to finish the legal process with me in court. Grey's birthfather had already signed and sent in the papers saying he "may" be the father, and that he did not wish to contest the adoption. I, on the other hand, was required to sit in the witness stand and testify in front of my mother, Sybil, and Ron—and a few random students taking notes in the back—concerning why I didn't want to parent this baby, physically point out the people who I did want to parent my child (like a victim points out her assailant in a trial), and finally was allowed to sign the papers, relinquishing my parental rights. I don't remember much about that morning, but I do remember wanting to ask the judge if he was out of his mind. Of course I wanted my baby; this had nothing to do with not wanting him. If this decision had anything to do with me, I would be home with my son right now! The whole thing felt degrading to me. As we walked out of the courtroom, in a rare moment of intimacy, my mother put her arm around me and said that I had just given this family a wonderful gift.

19

My Parents, Your Parents, the Birthparents

Helping friends and family understand open adoption is not always easy. Often there are people on both sides of the equation, birth and adoptive, who think it is a very bad idea. For the adoptive families, it is obvious why someone might think that. Wasn't there a very good reason that for so many years women never saw their babies again? Didn't that help them move on with their lives? Wouldn't seeing your baby again make you sad all over again and give you ideas about wanting him back? Wouldn't it be confusing to your child to have two mothers? After all, didn't you have to agree to all this just so you would be picked?

We left court that day and drove back to Sybil's parents' house where Grey was waiting. My mom and Sybil's mom made awkward small talk while I held Grey every minute I could. I definitely felt relieved to have the legalities done and settled, at least in my mind, but that didn't seem to make Sybil's mom any less uptight. I could see her point: we were definitely out of the closet for 1990, but I eventually realized that no matter how many years I was around, and no matter how much she got to know me, she would always be a little nervous about our open adoption.

When Grey was about seven years old, I happened to pull into

Sybil and Ron's driveway just as Sybil's mom was driving out. I asked if she had known I was coming. Sybil laughed and said, "Yes, she did," giving me the obvious impression that her mom's departure coinciding with my arrival wasn't exactly a coincidence.

I joked, "Hey, did you tell her that this time I was here to take him back?"

DEFINING FAMILY

Some people compare having a birth family in your life to having in-laws. You didn't choose them, you may not always like them, but you make it work because they came with someone you love. I guess that's not a completely terrible analogy, but then again, I know how some people feel about their in-laws! I'm sure it must be overwhelming to have a new baby and all the new responsibilities that come along with that, and at the same time, dump a new set of relationships with people you really hardly know, and some you may not particularly like, right into your lap.

Some adoptive families include their child's birthmother, and sometimes other members of the birth family, in their family events. Some never do. Many of my friends have been invited to their birth child's baptisms, which is often the first official event that includes any extended family members. It is awkward at first; there is a lot of whispering and secretive pointing among the relatives ("That's her, the birthmother"), but it also gives extended family a chance to see with their own eyes the woman who made all this possible and to give her a big hug and thank her personally. I know those moments make a big impact on everyone.

Even if it is awkward, and even if it is the only family gathering she ever attends, having your child's birthmother at an important event makes a strong statement to your extended family, whether they agree with the idea or not, that open adoption is for our child, and our child's birthmother is valuable.

Some birthmothers hit it off with their child's extended family and enjoy being invited to events. Maybe this surprises you, but it happens more than I would have guessed. Ron's extended family has that unmistakable Southern hospitality, which means they never meet a stranger. Even if they didn't like you one bit, you would never suspect! When I was still pregnant with Grey, they were the kindest, most generous people I could have ever imagined wanting around me. Ron's mom, although a bit blunt sometimes, wasn't at all afraid to talk to me about having Grey and why I thought that I wasn't going to change my mind and "break her baby's heart." I guess part of the reason I didn't change my mind was exactly because of that! Being deeply religious people, they all told me I would be rewarded for choosing to give my baby life. If for no other reason, they made me feel proud of myself at a time when pride was hard to come by.

Sybil's family, although always warmly welcoming, have a different family culture than Ron's. They are much more like my own frugal, conservative Dutch family. The general guideline for dealing with anything unpleasant in this culture is to just not talk about it and instead pretend it isn't there. I wouldn't go so far as to say they are rigid; just that emotions of any kind aren't really anyone's favorite topic. Sybil was never a big hugger, but I'd say that she's come a long way since she's known me!

Birthparents may often receive discouragement from their friends and family too—it just comes from a different vantage point. Every time you visit, you're a mess for days! Why would you put yourself through that? Isn't it like ripping the Band-Aid off the wound just as it was beginning to heal? Maybe you should just go on with your life and leave those poor people alone; after all, they adopted your baby—not you, too!

My parents have never quite embraced my open adoption in the same way as the rest of my family. Grey and his parents have always been welcomed at our family Christmas parties, and Grey has come to our cottage in the summer, but my parents, who don't live nearby, when given the chance to visit have opted out. I've tried to convince them that they wouldn't be viewed as an intrusion or that Ron and Sybil really do welcome more people to love Grey, but it just doesn't seem to change their uneasiness about this unorthodox approach to adoption.

WHAT YOU CAN SEE CAN HURT

One day when Grey was still young, I got a letter from Sybil. I was shocked to read that they had moved to Michigan and now lived in the same town where I had attended college. Sybil was sorry she hadn't had a chance to let me know sooner, but the move happened much faster than they were expecting. I had no idea they were even thinking about moving back to Michigan. Suddenly life had changed from me needing an airplane to go see Grey to only needing a half a tank of gas. I was absolutely ecstatic and completely terrified all at the same time!

My biggest fear was that I would lose all self-control and want to go see him all the time. It was easy to not have to worry about that when seeing him more than a couple times a year wasn't realistically an option, but how would I trust myself now? He was in full toddler mode by now, and I hadn't seen him for more than a year. I had a long visit when Grey was not yet one, barely a hello when he was almost two, and now he was almost three.

When I arrived to see Grey the first time since they moved, he was just waking from his nap, so Sybil went into his room to get him. I could hear her voice as she went in to wake him, "Grey . . . hey, Grey . . . guess who's here to see you?" She used this high-pitched, sing-songy voice, the kind of voice you use when you are waking up your kids on Christmas morning. It's the tone of voice that says, "Hey, there is something really cool to get excited about out here . . . wait until you see it!"

"Grey, come on and wake up! There's someone here to see you! Come on, come out and see who's here!"

Grey peeked his sleepy head around the corner with his blanket in his hand and his two fingers in his mouth. I hate to say it, but from the way his mom was talking, he must have thought that there was going to be something pretty great waiting for him in the living room, and turns out, it was just a strange lady who he didn't even know. *Where are the presents, anyway?*

Grey hid behind his mom's legs, shyly peeking out at me. This brown-eyed, beautiful, towheaded little boy looked even more like me in person than any picture could have ever led me to believe. He wasn't a baby anymore, but a little person. It was amazing.

And it was heartbreaking. I was a stranger. The little baby I'd baked in my belly, birthed, and loved with every cell in my body didn't know me.

It took him a long time to warm up to me, and I'm sure that he never understood what the big deal was. We hung out and played with his toys and had a really nice time, just the three of us. He showed me his favorite toy, Batman. Sybil said they thought he wanted a "blue swing" for Christmas, but he was really saying "Bruce Wayne"!—they never did understand him in time.

After a couple of hours, I left. It was such a relief for it to be so easy to go see him. Driving home I was overjoyed that Sybil and Ron would now be at my upcoming wedding, come to my house for dinner sometimes, and that I could ride horses with Sybil again. Interestingly, all my thoughts were about having the adults I loved and who loved me back in my life again. Was I glad to see Grey? Absolutely, without a doubt; but somehow Grey held a different reality for me now. He was a little man with preferences and personality, not the little baby that was so obviously, thanks to me, here in the world. Yes, I was his birthmother, but I knew that my role was going to feel very different than it did when I left that little baby in Florida. For at least a while, I'd just be some strange lady in the living room.

There is no magic to genetics. When you're a birthmother and your child falls and bumps his head, he runs to his mama. And that mama isn't you. When you haven't visited your child in a long time, you are a stranger. Even if you do visit often, if your child is going through typical stranger anxiety, you're still a stranger. It is very hard to come to the realization that you have much stronger feelings for your child than your child has for you. Even though Sybil did her very best to get Grey excited to see me (for my benefit, I'm sure), he still didn't run right up to me for a hug like my boys do now when I come home from a weekend away from them. It is so hard to want to scoop up your child and squeeze the stuffing out of him or her, but know that if you really did that, this little two-year-old would completely freak out, which would be a completely appropriate response!

I think it has a much bigger impact on the adoptive parents to see their child's birthmother again, after some time has passed, and be instantly reminded of how much the child resembles her (and not them). Sybil used to say that to me the very minute I walked in the door. I know it struck her every single time she saw me.

Many people think that if a birthmother gets to see her child, you shouldn't have a reason to be sad, as if seeing your child is all you are sacrificing in an adoption. I have also heard that we should just be grateful for what we've got, since our children's adoptive families don't have to be so nice to us; that we're lucky compared to other birthmothers who get nothing! It's kind of like that awful saying some parents used to say to their kids: "Stop crying or I'll give you something to cry about!"

Certainly, there is a tremendous sense of shame in closed adoptions that relates directly to not being allowed to see your child. It makes birthmothers feel that they are defective or dangerous in a way that they must not even be aware of. If this is true, then the converse of that, being allowed to see your child, must therefore mean that you are a better person than a birthmother who can't, right? Even though it is not a belief I say I consciously hold, I can see elements of truth in this from my own life. In the early years of my adoption, whenever I told people about Grey and my adoption plan for him, I was always quick to tack on, "but I still get to see him," as if that somehow proved I wasn't the same as one of those "bad" birthmothers who weren't allowed to ever see their child again. When I began to examine this behavior in myself, I realized that not only did being able to tell people that I still knew my son make me feel better about myself, it also made the person I was talking to seem visibly relieved and less uncomfortable in talking to me about it, too.

Among groups of birthmothers, too, there are unspoken messages about contact. Not that anyone would ever say this aloud, or really even admit to consciously believing it, but the belief that the more open your adoption is the better person you must be does exist. If you never had contact to begin with, there is a sense of clarity, because that is just the way it is, but if your child's adoptive family ended contact that you once enjoyed with your child, it is incredibly shameful—even though a birthmother rarely did anything to deserve it!

The Evan B. Donaldson Adoption Institute 2006 study, "Safeguarding the Rights and Well-Being of Birthparents in the Adoption Process," confirms this. Women who have the highest grief levels are those who placed their children with the understanding that they would have ongoing information, but the arrangement was cut off.

Such contact/information is the most important factor in facilitating birthparents' adjustment, but only a handfull of states have laws to enforce post-adoption contact agreements in infant adoptions. The fact remains that no matter how much contact a birthmother has, she will always worry that she will have it taken away—like a child losing dessert after dinner. After all, dessert is a privilege, not a right—right?

NEGOTIATING CONTACT

The first family party I was invited to after Ron and Sybil moved to Michigan was Grey's third birthday party. Sybil's family is very friendly—it's not that I ever felt that they didn't like me; I just don't think they knew what to make of me taking ten thousand photos of Grey, when to them it was just another birthday. And then there were my ten presents for their one; that might have made them feel a little awkward too! I wasn't uncomfortable at all; I thoroughly enjoyed the entire day. It didn't really matter to me what they thought; I was in heaven.

The next year around Grey's birthday, Sybil called, and I can't say I remember exactly how she pulled it off so smoothly, but it was masterful. She suggested we have our own little private birthday party together instead of me coming to the family party—except the way she proposed it made me feel that her suggestion was completely for my benefit alone, so I could have more uninterrupted time with Grey, not because my being at last year's family party made everyone else so uncomfortable! I don't think they asked to not have me there; I just think it was less stressful for Sybil to deal with. Whatever the case, I must say that it was a genius move on her part. Every year since, we've had our own party, and I wouldn't have wanted it any other way.

Prior to an adoption, most families' biggest concerns revolve around the fear that every time they open their front door, their child's birthmother will be sitting on their front stoop. They worry that she will want to come for Sunday brunch each week and on Thursday evenings for family game night.

What is reality for most adoptions is that the first year is awkward, visits are hard, and birthmothers find seeing their child both wonderful and intensely painful at the same time. This is likely followed by a period of time when she withdraws and is less likely to reach out and maybe won't want any contact at all for a while.

Finally, life becomes life again, and even though I would've never believed it would be possible, there did come a day when Sybil and I had to sync our calendars to plan a visit weeks in advance or it wouldn't happen. Just like everything else in life, blink and now he's an adult.

I would say that most people negotiate their relationships in naturally progressing degrees. Since many relationships begin without secrecy, there often aren't any big decisions about when to reveal a last name or address. If you begin building some traditions together, just as you would with any other members of your family, it will probably grow organically on its own. Just as we began celebrating Grey's birthday with our own little gathering, you may attend an annual festival together or go to the zoo every June. Whatever it is, make it practical and something fun for your child.

Ideally, contact should be a two-way street. Don't always wait for your child's birthmother to call you; I cannot tell you how often I hear that frustration from birthmothers! They never feel completely welcomed as a full member of the relationship if they are always the ones initiating the contact. It is an exciting day for a birthmother the first time her child's parent calls her for no reason, just to see how she is doing or to ask her to meet for lunch. It really indicates a relationship transforming from one of "the only reason we know each other is because I am pregnant with this baby" to one where we are two individuals and friends, as well as birthmother to your child. It is often a relief to sense some balance entering the interaction.

20

The Brother from Another Mother: Siblings

The issues surrounding siblings have traditionally been largely ignored in adoption. Siblings, much like the adopted person himself, have no say in the events but must still deal with the changes that those events bring to his life.

It might surprise you to learn that more than half of expectant mothers making an adoption plan are already parenting other children. These women have concerns that someone planning an adoption for their first baby does not. If the child she is already parenting is too young to be cognizant of the pregnancy, she might not be forced to deal with her child's needs until later than if her child clearly understands the events as they are happening. Even a very young child will sense the turmoil of an expectant mother's grief, so she needs to be aware that her struggles will affect her child, too. Adoption is like a pebble thrown into still water—its ripples extend out a very long way.

A very important part in counseling expectant mothers who are already parents is to give them the tools they need to help the child that is already here, as well as the one who isn't yet. Often it's not that they don't want to talk to their child about their adoption plan, it is just that they don't know how, so when you help them with the right words to say, they feel relieved. Now that I am a parent myself, I understand firsthand how hard this is. It is very similar to what adoptive parents go through in explaining the concept of being adopted to their child. You start with basic, concrete information, and as your child grows, that information must too.

There is a wonderful children's book called *Sam's Sister*, by Juliet Bond, that is intended to help expectant mothers explain their adoption plan to their children and to help them understand what to expect. If you connect with an expectant mother who is already parenting a young child, I highly recommend you give her a copy of this book.

WHAT TO SAY

One of the biggest anxieties for an expectant mother is not knowing how to approach the topic of her adoption plan with her child. An expectant mother may believe that because her existing child has never brought it up, he must not have noticed her stomach growing bigger each day. Even when it is obvious that a child knows his mother is pregnant, if she doesn't bring it up, her child probably won't either. Her biggest fear—that her child will be hurt because of the adoption—is often legitimate, and one that is sometimes, sadly, unavoidable.

I advise women first and foremost to tell their child the truth, and tell it using terminology that their child can understand. Here is an example of some dialog that I might use: "Yes, there is a baby growing inside mommy's tummy, and that baby is your little sister. When your sister comes out of my tummy, I have picked another mommy and daddy for her, and she is going to live with them at their house forever and ever. This is called 'adoption.' Their names are Miss Sarah and Mr. David, and you are going to meet them with me today.

"When your sister comes out of my tummy, I will go to the hospital and Grandma will come stay with you. She will bring you to the hospital to visit me and to meet your new sister. We will take pictures of you holding your baby sister, and they will be your special pictures to keep wherever you want. After two 'sleeps,' I will come home and be your mommy forever and ever, and Miss Sarah and Mr. David will be your sister's mommy and daddy forever and ever.

"We will get to visit her sometimes and even bring her a present on her birthday. Sometimes we will miss her and it will be sad for both of us that she doesn't live at our house. I might cry and you might cry, and that is okay too. She is going to be safe and happy, and we can smile when we remember that."

This short conversation is packed full of important details:

- She refers to the baby as her son's sister. This gives her child permission to claim this baby as family, as well as giving him a way to refer to her that he can understand.
- She also gives her child names to call the adoptive parents. This is something you can talk about in advance and all agree on. Notice that their names aren't "mom and dad" to him, even though they will be to his new baby sister, and this introduces that difference right away.
- Notice she waited to tell her child about Miss Sarah and Mr. David until after she has already met them and is sure they are the family she would like to adopt her baby.
- She also waited to tell her child about the meeting until the actual day it will happen. For young children, time is a difficult concept to measure, and telling them anything too far in advance is confusing.
- She included some concrete details that we, as adults, would simply assume, but a concrete-thinking child needs to have spelled out: his sister will live at Miss Sarah and Mr. David's house, not at his house, and she will live there forever. Explaining that this is a permanent arrangement is critical,

because many children naturally believe that after some period of time their sibling will come back to live with them. They also need to be reassured, many times, that their role in their own family is secure, and that they will not be going to live with any other mommy and daddy too. After all, if your sibling can be adopted, then why not you too?

■ She prepares him for the fact that she will need to go to the hospital and that his grandma will come care for him. If she had only talked about adoption and a new mommy and daddy, and then suddenly disappeared for two days, you can see how a child may think she was not coming back. I always found using the number of "sleeps" until an event was helpful to explain time to my kids.

■ She lets him know that he will get to meet his sister, hold her, and visit her in the future. Using an example of a birthday can be useful because it may help illustrate the difference between what this relationship will be like, where the visits are arranged in advance, rather than simply just dropping by anytime, like you might a friend or neighbor's house.

■ Last, she lets him know that she will be sad and that it is okay if he is sad too. His mom's tears won't alarm him if he expects them, and she won't have to worry about hiding them from him either. She also tells him that there are things to be happy about as well, and that they will smile too; this "bittersweetness" is hard for many adults to understand, but luckily, a concrete-thinking child will not be phased if you tell him it's perfectly normal.

EXPLAINING THE WHYS

What was not included in this dialogue were all her reasons for not choosing to parent her new baby. For a very young child, the concrete details of what is happening will be enough, but when a child is older, she will need to offer some explanations concerning the "why" part. Obviously, a child will not have an adult understanding of what it really means to be a parent, so the child may try to offer solutions that seem perfectly logical to them. If a mom tells a six-year-old that she does not have enough money to take care of another baby, he may offer to eat less, or promise to help her with the baby, or get a job to make more money. If she says that she wants her baby to have both a mommy and a daddy, her son may say that they can just find someone else to be the daddy, not understanding what this really means.

One birthmother's seven-year-old daughter offered to babysit so her mom could go to work. Expectant mothers need to understand that her answers during the "why" conversations will change and evolve over time as her child gets older, and as hard as it is, she will never be able to completely shield her child from this loss.

As my boys grew older and began to understand more about their brother Grey, I started explaining to them the "why" reasons for his adoption. First I said it was because "Grey's mommy's tummy was broken and couldn't have babies. So when I had a baby and wasn't ready to be a mommy, I chose them to be Grey's mommy and daddy. . . ." This seemed to satisfy them for quite a while, until one day out of the blue, Asher, a very sensitive child, said to me, "Mom, I wish that lady's tummy wasn't broken so Grey could have lived here with us."

Of course, this was hard to hear, but I also knew (in my head, at least) that it was okay for Asher to have his own grief, and the best thing I could do was to help him process it. So I took the explanation a step further by adding that, "I wasn't ready to be a mommy, and if Grey's mommy didn't have a broken tummy, I still would have wanted to find another mommy and daddy for Grey."

I also let him know that I feel exactly the same way too sometimes. When I asked him what made him think of that, he said, "I dunno. I just wish sometimes that I had an older brother." I quickly affirmed that he still does have an older brother and was he just missing him? Since I couldn't change the fact that Grey didn't live with us, I did what I could do, which was to arrange a time for us to go visit.

INVOLVING OLDER KIDS

When an expectant mother is parenting an older child or children, sometimes they are actively involved with their mother's adoption plans. This can be a healthy way for the entire family to become empowered in making a good decision for their sibling, which will also help them grieve that loss more fully down the road as well.

One caution: siblings, no matter how old, need to understand that the ultimate decisions made are not up to them, but will be made by the adult(s) involved, which usually means their mother. It is great to let them read profiles and meet the family that everyone liked best, but they still need to know that they do not have the power (nor must they bear the burden) of making these hugely impacting decisions. If a parent leans too much on their child for input, emotional support, or even asks for their advice, the roles become confused and the child may feel responsible for the parent's grief.

When there are older siblings already present, it is important that you, the prospective adoptive parent, try to include them in whatever way you can. Ask the expectant mother to tell you all about them; a mother can never talk too much about her kids, and this can strike up any number of conversations. It also shows her that you are interested in more than just the baby she is carrying. Find out what her older child enjoys and arrange an outing for all of you. When the baby is born, bring a small gift not just for the birthmother, but for her current child as well.

If you do some kind of placement ceremony, include the siblings as well. If they are older, ask them to write a letter or draw a picture to send with their new sibling. Choose a gift that symbolizes your new relationship. Their very own photo album or picture frame is always a great idea whether it is a boy or a girl. One adoptive father created a ritual especially for the three older sons that their child's birthmother was already parenting. It symbolized that they were all family now and that they would always be together even if separated by a long distance. This small gesture made a huge impact on the brothers. It included them in the adoption and reinforced that they were a valuable part of their sibling's life. Though they still struggled with grief, as anyone would, the ritual reassured them that adoption was the best choice.

TAKE NOTE

Don't forget that you are hoping to adopt a baby who is genetically related to these siblings, and you can certainly gain some valuable insight into your own child from getting to know them. The tapestry of nature and nurture is a fascinating one to see, and I can tell you that sometimes the cloth is too tightly woven to see exactly where the thread originated from.

Around the time that my son Isaac was three, I privately referred to him as "my little do-over." His voice and mannerisms were so strikingly like Grey's that often I would be instantly overwhelmed with emotion. In some ways I felt as if I were being given a chance to have back what I had missed by not parenting Grey. Obviously, Isaac is not Grey in many other ways too, but I certainly would not have predicted that the two half brothers would look a thousand times more alike than my two full-blood siblings do.

Don't underestimate the relationship your child may have someday with his or her biological siblings. Often adopted people are not nearly as interested in searching for their birthparents as they are in finding any siblings they may have. Siblings often aren't the recipients of many of the complicated feelings that an adopted person may have for their birthparents. Even if you think they will never have anything in common or too much economic disparity to ever become friends, don't be too sure.

WHEN SIBLINGS COME LATER

It wasn't until ten years later that I became a parent myself. When I found out I was pregnant, one of the first people I wanted to tell was Grey. When I called and told him that I was going to have a baby, he yelled to his mom, "Hey, Mom! I'm going to have another brother!" Interestingly, I didn't use the word "brother"; he claimed that all on his own. (Even though, apparently, the thought that it might be a sister hadn't ever occurred to him!)

It felt very important to me that I honor Grey in some way to show that even though I had more children, he was still my firstborn and that this bond was sacred. We named our son Asher Grey, and to this day, my favorite photo of all time is one of Grey holding baby Asher for the very first time. For some reason, that photo feels to me like the closing of so many incomplete circles for all of us.

I have a new favorite memory. We recently visited Grey at college, and as we were saying good-bye and giving hugs, Asher (who is now nine years old) looked at Grey (who is now nineteen), and said, "I love ya, bro."

The roots of our families' trees can grow very, very deep, providing more than enough strength and stability in its branches to hold all the ones we love.

21

"Hey, World, I'm A Dopted!"

There are many very good resources out there to help you talk to your child about being adopted, and there are also some really terrible ones. (You can find a list of my favorites in the resource section at the back of this book.) One of the best ways to get good ideas about this topic is to talk to other adoptive parents, and—as obvious as this is going to seem—talk to your child. After all, you have the resident expert right there under your own roof, and if you aren't taking advantage of private consultations, you are probably making things much harder for yourself than they need to be!

PRACTICE

After becoming a parent, I realized right away that actually saying the words aloud to my child was one billion times harder than saying the same words to anyone else in the whole world. For someone who drones on about this all the time—can't shut up about it, in fact—I still find that I have a lump in my throat when it isn't a room of five hundred people but my own precious child asking the hard questions. Even I had to practice hearing myself saying the things I would need to say to my kids. The more I said them, the easier it got and the better I got at it. It's also ironic that as you become more relaxed about it all, your child will sense that it is okay to strike up a conversation. When you're all worked up about it, worrying that your child is going to bring up some horrifying adoption question, don't worry—they probably won't, because kids know what makes you freak out.

BRING IT UP

Everybody has something that, growing up in their family, they just knew they should not bring up, because if they did, it made their mom or dad extremely uncomfortable. Even though it was never said aloud that "We don't talk about that," they just sensed the tension and knew that was a topic to avoid.

Adoption and birthparents can become taboo subjects if you allow them to. I think the two easiest mistakes to make in this area are: (1) waiting for your child to bring up the topic, and (2) thinking that you must have all the right answers ready and waiting (or, of course, you're a bad parent!).

There are so many great children's books now about adoption. My boys love to read *Sam's Sister*; even though it doesn't completely reflect their own experience, it still affirms so much of what they, too, have felt at some time or another. When children are very small, you can practice telling them their adoption story just to hear yourself saying it; they won't know or remember, but it is an excellent way for you to make it less awkward for yourself.

Having a photo of your child's birthmother on display in your home gives your child a powerful message that this person is not only important, but that it is okay to talk about her. It will also force you to have to talk about her from time to time when other adults ask, "Who is that in that photo?"

When kids are going through what I like to call the "myna bird phase"—you know, when they repeat everything they've heard to every stranger they meet—telling everyone that they're adopted will likely be one of those things too. Kids can't differentiate why it's okay to talk about it at home but not to talk about it with the nice lady in the cereal aisle. If that happens, embarrassing as it might be, take heart that you are doing your job well!

The easiest way I've found to bring up the topic of adoption with my boys as they get older is to just let them in on my thoughts. If Isaac does or says something that reminds me of his brother, sometimes I will tell him that. "You know what? When you laughed like that, you sounded just like your older brother Grey." This doesn't begin an epic conversation or anything; in fact, he doesn't really seem to care at all. But if you asked him who he looks like, he will tell you he looks and acts a lot like his oldest brother, Grey.

If you happen to be thinking about your child's birthmother, say that. "You know what? I was just thinking about Susie today. I wonder how she is doing? Do you ever wonder that too?" If you are coloring pictures with your child, send one to Grandma and ask if she would like you to send one to her birthmother too. That's as strong a statement as anything you can say with words to your child.

When Grey was small, I had no idea what to expect when I visited him. I was always terrified that it would be during this visit that he would ask me the "big one." You know, why did I give him away, or didn't I love him, or was he an ugly baby and that's why I didn't want him? Not yet being a parent myself, I had no idea what he understood or didn't understand; it would have been enormously helpful for Sybil to let me know the kinds of things he was talking about.

During one visit, Grey was about five, and we were in the barn visiting one of Sybil's horses who was going to have a baby soon. As we stood there together, Grey looked over at me and said, "Do you have any babies?" I was petrified and caught so off guard that I didn't know how to answer. "Well, uh, no, sweetie, not yet." Later, of course, I was kicking myself for not answering with one of those perfect social worker answers that I was always coaching my clients on: "Of course I did, silly, I had you!" or, "You grew in my tummy, remember?"

I was also—how shall I put this—exasperated that Sybil was obviously not telling Grey about his adoption adequately. Sybil (a little defensive, not that I could blame her) told me to relax, that he just didn't understand the whole baby thing yet and got a little confused about babies growing in tummies, where they end up, and what that means. I don't think I was convinced at the time, but I know now that she was right on.

One adoptive mother talked about her adopted son trying to sort out the differences between his brother, who joined their family by birth, and his own.

"Mom, let me get this straight. Brian grew in your tummy, right?"

"Right."

"And I grew in Christina's tummy, and you adopted me, right?"

"Right."

"Then Mom . . . why are you Brian's mom?"

When I was pregnant with Asher, Grey asked Sybil if my baby was going to come live with them. No one had ever told him that they wouldn't be adopting all my babies, so he just wanted to check. Different kids figure it out in different ways, and I think if I tried to analyze everything that comes out of my boys' mouths, I could probably find a pathogenic label for just about everything they say!

GIVING YOUR KIDS THE WORDS

Helping kids learn the right words to describe their reality is ultimately giving them the empowerment to choose to share (or to not share) that story with others.

I walked up behind my son Asher, then eight, while he was

huddled in a little group talking to some of his friends. I realized after a second that the subject of this animated conversation was whether or not he really did have an older brother. Since he didn't see me come up, I decided to listen in for a minute. Obviously, this conversation had already been going on for a few minutes, because the conversation was heating up, with Asher saying quite insistently, "Yes, I really DO have another brother."

"Then how come I've never seen him?"

"I told you, he doesn't live with me because he was adopted."

"What? Isaac was adopted? I didn't know that!"

"No, not Isaac! My other brother. My older brother was adopted, not Isaac."

"Well, if he was adopted, then why doesn't he live with you?"

"Because I told you, when you are adopted, you live with the people who adopt you, duh!"

I realized that this wasn't getting any better and probably wouldn't without a little assistance. When Asher saw me, his face lit up and he immediately said, "Mom! Hey, tell them that I do have another brother, a brother named Grey and that he was adopted. I keep trying to tell them what adoption is, but they don't get it!" Even though I thought I had given Asher all the words he needed to accurately tell his story, apparently I hadn't gotten quite far enough.

LEARNING TO GO WITH THE FLOW

Now that Grey is older, I have had to learn to let him handle our relationship in whatever way he wants. Sometimes that can end up being a little awkward for me. When he was a teenager and working as a summer camp counselor, he asked over and over if I would bring Asher and Isaac to visit him there. We finally found a couple of free days to come for what I thought would be just "hanging out." As soon as we arrived, Grey began walking us around and introducing us to everyone at the camp. I could tell from the way he was talking and the knowing looks I was getting that he had been talking about us already—a lot! A couple of adults even approached me on their own and said, "I'm guessing you must be Grey's birthmother, since you look just like him." And, "We knew you were coming; we've heard a lot about you."

Okay, just what does that mean? You heard so much about me, like so much good, bad, or crazy about me? Has Grey been emotionally barfing up adoption pain all summer and I had no idea? As the weekend progressed, I began to feel much better about the situation and figured out that all my fear was really my own insecurities coming out. It seemed that Grey was just very proud to have us there and really wanted all his friends to meet us. Someone said to me that they thought it was "so cool how Grey could know us and it was no big deal."

Sometimes as an adult, Grey might introduce me as his mom, rather than his birthmom, which I have to tell you is hard for me. When I asked him about it, it was obvious that he just doesn't always feel like explaining it to everyone and eventually they will figure it out anyway. It isn't a slight to Sybil in any way (unless her not looking like him is a deliberate slight, I guess). You can tell when we're together that people look at him and then look at me, and they've already assumed we are related in some way, so to introduce me as a friend would be even harder for him to try to explain. I'd say that Grey is pretty grounded and that his parents have done a great job of helping him know all the different parts of himself. Even those of us who weren't adopted struggle with similar issues, which is easy to forget sometimes. I try to defer to what he needs and wants, and unless it is something totally crazy, I'll just try to go with the flow.

I often think back to that night when Sybil asked, "Who makes these rules?" Well, I guess now that person is Grey.

22

Birthmothering

It's the "forever" part of being a birthmother that is so much harder than I expected. After the crying stopped, I began to feel so much better. I knew things were improving the day that I suddenly stopped dead in my tracks, standing in my kitchen looking in the freezer for something for dinner, when I realized that I hadn't thought about Grey even once that day. That was zero, down from one gazillion times a day! I felt a huge surge of guilt—how could I forget about my child? I must be the worst person ever! I know now that this moment was a signal, not that I was forgetting about Grey, but rather that I was integrating the role of birthmom into my life. It was becoming just a part of who I am, instead of being the overwhelming whole. I hate the phrase "moving on" with your life in respect to adoption; I prefer "moving it into" your life.

It takes a long time and a lot of work—much more work than I expected. Sometimes the work was just allowing time to pass and allowing myself to be happy sometimes and sometimes not, while other times the work was me needing to make very deliberate decisions.

When Grey was small, I hated the way Sybil dressed him. Don't worry, it's no secret, and we've laughed about it plenty, but until he was about five years old, every time I had an occasion to buy him a gift (which was just about every time I saw him), I included outfits that were clearly my taste, not Sybil's. This issue was the first thing I recognized as being something I needed to let go of, because clearly, I had no right to it and it was stopping me from having peace. I made a conscious decision to not buy clothing for Grey anymore, which for me was extremely hard (and extremely shallow!) but very valuable in my integration process.

When I say that I wish for birthmothers to find peace, I don't mean that they never feel sad again, but rather that they are able to integrate their "birthmotherness" into their lives as a balanced part of who they are: a valuable, meaningful, and portioned part of one's identity.

WHAT ABOUT THE AGENCIES?

There are many struggles birthmothers face, but unfortunately, there aren't nearly enough supports out there to expect that they will handle them well. As it is, there are few resources for adoptive parents, but there are almost zero for birthparents. It is easy for us, as professionals, to say that "open adoption is best for children," but it is completely unfair and unrealistic for us to expect that birthparents will be helpful participants in those relationships without anyone teaching them what that means! The way I see the current system of open adoption is that it very often sets people up for failure.

One big reason birthmothers do not return to their placing agencies for post-placement support (aside from the fact that there is rarely any offered) is because they view the agency as having been biased to the adoptive families. Adoptive families pay the fees that operate the agency, which leaves some birthmothers feeling like a commodity rather than a person. Often, the very issues they are struggling to deal with were caused by the agency itself; they later learned that they weren't told the whole truth by the agency, or that they weren't advocated for as they should have been, or they weren't given all the options to choose from in their adoption planning. If a birthmother does go back for support, often the professional who helped her with her placement and knows her is no longer employed there.

Then there is the conflict agencies run up against by having been the good cop and the bad cop in an adoption. As hard as it was for me to hear, there were many times that birthmothers just did not want to talk to me after an adoption, because I was the one who personally facilitated her signing the surrender papers. It is hard to separate the advocacy from the adversary when they were actually the same person!

I don't feel guilty about having taken adoption surrenders with birthmothers, but it helps that I worked for an agency that had the utmost integrity about letting a birthmother call the shots in her own plan, not the other way around. The directors, who were also my mentors, often defended my decisions to the prospective adoptive parents when placements didn't proceed as smoothly or as quickly as they would have liked. Not every adoption counselor I know has had the same experience. It wasn't uncommon for my colleagues to feel pressure, spoken or unspoken, to make placements happen.

CONNECTION = COMMUNITY

There are many excellent organizations that help adoptive parents and families to connect, learn, and support each other on all kinds or adoption-related topics. Some groups are more informal, maybe just a playgroup or a mom's group, but many are part of a larger network and have regular social events, conferences, and regular newsletters to help you feel supported when you encounter a rough patch. I wish that some of these groups would expand to include the birthparent as a valued member in need of support. I think families would be surprised by how many birthmothers there are who have questions and would like to know how to strengthen their adoption relationships. Because there are so few role models for birthmothers to look to for guidance, some women feel isolated in their birthmother role for their whole lives.

One of the most valuable functions of any group is that they simply connect people to other people like them. Isolation has such damaging effects for birthmothers; it increases her shame, which then bleeds over and affects so many other areas in her life. When one birthmother meets another for the first time, the effect is remarkable. Just as one breast cancer survivor knows what another has experienced without even knowing her story, all birthmothers share common bonds that are that powerful. I am proud to be a part of that connecting movement.

ON YOUR FEET

In 2001, I was honored to be asked to help start the On Your Feet Foundation, the very first organization in the United States that exists solely to assist birthparents. Often the goals we help them reach are the same things lacking in their lives that greatly influenced their decision to make an adoption plan to begin with. We raise money to provide grants for college, job training, counseling, or life coaching.

Since 2003, a unique part of our support and education has been through biannual weekend retreats for birthmothers. Along with my friend and colleague, Cher Pollock, we have had the honor of welcoming hundreds of birthmothers from all over the country to retreats that we call "On Your Feet for Life." Aside from educating and giving women a safe place to share, the retreats have created a sisterhood that extends far beyond the weekend retreats. Many of the birthmothers who were once recipients of grants themselves have now become our next generation of donors.

Because we aren't affiliated with any adoption agency or placing organization of any kind, there is no mixed message about what we do and why we exist. Ultimately, our goal is to strengthen adoptive families, which includes our children. My dream is to see us reproduce, as we have once already with On Your Feet of Northern California. (Since we birthmothers do have a proven track record in the expertise of reproduction, we ought to be able to do this, don't you think?) We have a long way to go, but when the message finally gets out and the shadows are scattered, you will see that strong and beautiful birthmothers are already where you least expected to find them—just about everywhere!

IN IT FOR THE LONG HAUL

Now that Grey is an adult, being his birthmom is in some ways much harder. I don't know if it is much different than any parent watching their child try to figure out what he wants to be when he grows up, but for the first time I worry that even his parents can't protect him from these hard knocks. That is a new one for me.

I can tell you that my relationship with Grey is stronger and closer than I ever imagined it would be, but then again, it is also so unremarkable that people never seem to stop being surprised. I am just his birthmother, no one special, really; I've always been around and probably always will be. I visited him at college recently and brought him a care package of groceries just as any mom would. Do I slip him some cash like my father did, when I was in college? No way—that's his parents' job.

I don't talk to Sybil and Ron nearly as much as I used to. Now when we talk, it is more like catching up than anything else. Sometimes I think I know Grey better than they do, but that really isn't that unusual when you're talking about a teenager and his parents, is it? I still feel a strong allegiance to them, and I probably always will. If Grey were ever headed for trouble, I would be the first person on the phone telling them.

I'm starting to think about the next phase in this unusual relationship and wonder what it will be like. What if I don't like who he chooses to marry? What about when he has kids? How does a birth grandma fit in? Or will I at all?

I know there is a tremendous amount of pressure on many adopted people that they don't do anything in terms of a relationship with their birthparents that would hurt their adoptive parents. The perception is that if you need a relationship with your birthparents, your adoptive parents must not have been wholly parents, which just isn't true. I have a hard time imagining Ron or Sybil being threatened by anything I would do, since there really hasn't ever been an "us" and a "them." I tell Grey just about every time I see him that I love his parents, I picked them, and that makes us all on the same team: Team Grey.

Selected References

References are listed in order of appearance.

Herman, Ellen. "Adoption History Project." University of Oregon. Accessed online at http://www.uoregon.edu/~adoption/index.html.

Fessler, Anne. *The Girls Who Went Away: The Hidden History of Women Who Surrendered Children for Adoption in the Decades Before Roe v. Wade.* Penguin, 2007.

Carney, Eliza Newlin. "Perception and Reality: The Untold Story of Domestic Adoption." *Adoptive Families* magazine. 2009. Accessed online at http://www.adoptivefamilies.com/articles.php?aid=1618.

Bachrach, Christine, Patricia Adams, Soledad Sambrano, and Kathryn London. "Adoption in the 1980s." *Advance Data from Vital and Health Statistics of the National Center for Health Statistics*, no. 181 (January 1990): 6. U.S. Department of Health and Human Services. [*Author's note*: Eight percent of all adoptions included parents and children of different races.]

Petition of Doe. 159 Ill. 2d 347, 202 Ill. Dec. 535, 638 N.E.2d 181, 1994.

Clausen (Deboer v. Schmidt), 502 N.W.2d 649, Mich. 1993.

Evan B. Donaldson Adoption Institute. "National Adoption Attitudes Survey." Evan B. Donaldson Adoption Institute. Accessed online at http://www.adoptioninstitute.org/survey/Adoption_Attitudes_Survey.pdf.

Grotevant, Harold, and Ruth G. McRoy, directors. Minnesota/Texas Adoption Research Project. Accessed online at http://www.cehd.umn.edu/fsos/Centers/mtarp.

Evan B. Donaldson Adoption Institute. 2006. "Safeguarding the Well-Being of Birthparents in the Adoption Process." Accessed online at http://www.adoptioninstitute.org/publications.

American Adoptions. "This Is Your Choice." 1996–2000. Accessed online at http://www.americanadoptions.com/pregnant/article_view/article_id/3209?cId=49.

Gritter, James. *Lifegivers: Framing the Birthparent Experience in Open Adoption*. Washington, D.C.: CWLA Press, 2000, 2–3.

Melina, Lois Ruskai, and Sharon Kaplan Roszia. *The Open Adoption Experience: A Complete Guide for Adoptive and Birth Families*. HarperCollins, 1993.

Spence-Chapin Adoptions. "A Birthparents Bill of Rights." Accessed online at http://www.spence-chapin.org/downloads/BillORights-2008_English.pdf.

Jones, Jo. "Who Adopts? Characteristics of Women and Men Who Have Adopted Children." National Center for Health Statistics Data Brief 5, no. 12 (2009). Accessed online at http://www.cdc.gov/nchs/data/databriefs/db12.pdf.

Evan B. Donaldson Adoption Institute. 2008. "Expanding Resources for Waiting Children II: Eliminating Legal and Practice Barriers to Gay and Lesbian Adoption from Foster Care Policy and Practice Perspective." Accessed online at http://www.adoptioninstitute.org/policy/2008_09_expand_resources.php.

IRS. June 2008. Publication 557, "Tax-Exempt Status For Your Organization," 65–66. Cat. No. 46573C. Accessed online at http://www.irs.gov/pub/irs-pdf/p557.pdf.

Association of Administrators of the Interstate Compact on the Placement of Children. "Interstate Compact for the Placement of Children: A Side-by-Side Comparison of the New and Current ICPC." Accessed online http://www.aphsa.org/Policy/icpc2006.

American Academy of Adoption Attorneys. Accessed online at http://www.adoption.

Wolff, Jana. *Secret Thoughts of an Adoptive Mother*. Kansas City, MO, Andrews and McMeel, 1997.

Bond, Juliet C. *Sam's Sister*. Indianapolis, IN, Perspectives Press, 2004.

Recommended Resources

CATALOGS AND WEBSITES
SPECIALIZING IN ADOPTION BOOKS

AdoptionBooks.com, http://www.adoptionbooks.com.
Adopt Shoppe, http://www.adoptshoppe.com.
Perspectives Press, http://www.perspectivespress.com.
Tapestry Books, http://www.tapestrybooks.com.

MAGAZINES

Adoptive Families magazine (print copy). Website: http://www.adoptive
    families.com/articles.php?aid=1618.
Adoption Today (digital magazine) at http://www.adoptiontoday.com
    or www.adoptinfo.net.

RECOMMENDED GROUPS AND WEBSITES

Adoption History Project. A wonderful compilation about the his-
    tory of adoption by the University of Oregon. Website: http://www.
    uoregon.edu/~adoption/index.html.

American Adoption Congress. Dedicated to education and advocacy in adoption. Website: http://www.americanadoptioncongress.org.

Ethica: An Independent Voice for Ethical Adoption. Website: http://www.ethicanet.org.

Evan B. Donaldson Adoption Institute. A good resource for research, statistics, and adoption information. Website: http://www.adoptioninstitute.org/index.php.

Happy Hour Mom. A blog for all moms with regular adoption articles (contributed by me!). Website: http://www.happyhourmom.com.

PACT: An Adoption Alliance. Adoption education and resources. www.pactadopt.org.

BOOKS (MY FAVORITES!)

Memoirs

Fessler, Ann. *The Girls Who Went Away: The Hidden History of Women Who Surrendered Children for Adoption in the Decades Before Roe v. Wade.* Penguin, 2006.

Franklin, Lynn. *May the Circle Be Unbroken: An Intimate Journey into the Heart of Adoption.* Authors Choice Press, 2005.

Koenig, Mary Ann, with photography by Niki Berg. *Sacred Connections: Stories of Adoption.* Running Press, 2000.

Phillips, Zara H. *Mother Me.* Gemma Media, 2011.www.gemmamedia.com.

Wolff, Jana. *Secret Thoughts of an Adoptive Mother.* Vista Communications, 1999.

Nonfiction/Adoption Education

Brodzinsky, David, Marshall D. Schecter, and Robin Marantz Henig. *Being Adopted: The Lifelong Search for Self.* Anchor, 1993.

Dorner, Patricia Martinez. *How to Open an Adoption: A Guide for Parents and Birthparents of Minors.* R-Squared Press, 1997.

Gritter, James. *Lifegivers: Framing the Birthparent Experience in Open Adoption.* CWLA Press, 1999.

Melina, Lois Ruskai. *Making Sense of Adoption: A Parent's Guide.* HarperCollins, 1989.

Melina, Lois Ruskai, and Sharon Kaplan Roszia. *The Open Adoption Experience: A Complete Guide for Adoptive and Birth Families.* HarperCollins, 1993.

Pavao, Joyce. *The Family of Adoption—Revised Edition.* Beacon Press, 2005.

Fiction

Larkin, Alison. *The English American.* Simon and Schuster, 2009.

Movies/Television

Lee, Barb, and Nancy Kim Parsons. *Adopted.* Documentary. See www.adoptedthemovie.com.

Opper, Nicole. *Off And Running: An American Coming of Age Story.* See www.offandrunningthefilm.com

Phillips, Zara. *Roots Unknown: A Film About Adoption.* See www.zarahphillips.com.

Strauss, Jean. *For the Life of Me.* Documentary. See www.jeanstrauss.com.

16 and Pregnant. Season 1. "Catelynn" episode. MTV, 2009. See http://www.mtv.com.

Teen Mom. Season 1. Episode 5. "A Little Help." MTV, 2009. See http://www.mtv.com.

Index

About the Author

Jennifer Joyce Pedley, MJ, is a birthmother and social worker who has been helping people build their families through adoption since 1995. It was her own personal experience of placing her son in an open adoption, following his birth in 1990, which prompted her to become a social worker and make the field of adoption her primary professional focus.

In addition to being a regular speaker at conferences all over the U.S., Pedley is a founding board member of the On Your Feet Foundation, the first of its kind, not-for-profit organization established in 2001 to provide ongoing support to birthparents. In 2003 she established and began co-facilitating therapeutic weekend retreats for birthmothers. One 2010 retreat was featured on MTV as a part of their documentary reality show *Teen Mom*. To date, these retreats have engaged hundreds of birthmothers from all over the United States.

Pedley lives in Michigan with her husband and two young sons. She continues to maintain close ties to her birth son as well as with his adoptive family.